Véronique Tadjo  0

writes and illustrates children's books. Born in Paris, of an Ivorian father and a French mother, she was brought up in Abidjan (Côte d'Ivoire). She has a doctorate in African American literature and civilization from the Sorbonne Paris IV. She was a Fulbright scholar at Howard University in Washington, DC and has travelled extensively in West Africa, Europe, USA and Latin America. She taught at the University of Abidjan for several years. She has conducted workshops on writing (and book illustration) in numerous countries. She has published several books and her novel *Reine Pokou* was awarded the prestigious literary prize "Grand Prix Littéraire d'Afrique Noire" in 2005. She has facilitated writing workshops for the Caine Prize for African Writing and has been a member of the jury for several literary prizes. Her books have been translated into several languages. She is Head of French Studies in the School of Literature & Language Studies, University of Witwatersrand in Johannesburg.

About the Translator

Amy Baram Reid is associate professor of French at New College of Florida, where she also directs the programme in Gender Studies. She holds a PhD. in French from Yale University and studied as well at the Ecole Normale Supérieure in Paris. She has published essays on 19th- and 20th-century literature, ranging from the Goncourts and J.-K. Huysmans to Anne Hébert and Véronique Tadjo. Her recent translations include *Dog Days: An Animal Chronicle* (University of Virginia Press, 2006), [*Temps de Chien*] by the Cameroonian author Patrice Nganang, as well as short stories by Tadjo and Nganang included in the anthology *From Africa: New Francophone* Stories (University of Nebraska Press, 2004).

First published in French as *Reine Pokou: Concerto pour un sacrifice*, Actes Sud 2004

This edition first published in English by Ayebia Clarke Publishing Limited 2009
7 Syringa Walk
Banbury
OX16 1FR
Oxfordshire
UK

Distributed outside Africa, Europe and the United Kingdom and in the USA exclusively by
Lynne Rienner Publishers Inc.
1800 30th St., Ste. 314
Boulder, CO 80301
USA
www.rienner.com

Co-published in Ghana with the Centre for Intellectual Renewal
56 Ringway Estate, Osu, Accra, Ghana.

British Library Cataloguing-in-Publication Data.
Cover Painting by Véronique Tadjo
Cover Design by Amanda Carroll at Millipedia.
Typeset by FiSH Books, Enfield, Middlesex.
Printed and bound in the UK by Cox & Wyman Ltd., Reading, Berkshire

ISBN 978-0-9555079-9-1

Distributed in Africa, Europe and the UK by TURNAROUND Publisher Services at
www.turnaround-uk.com

Also available from www.ayebia.co.uk or email info@ayebia.co.uk

The Publisher wishes to acknowledge the support of Arts Council SE Funding.

QUEEN POKOU

Concerto for a sacrifice

By Véronique Tadjo

Translated from the French
by Amy Baram Reid

An Adinkra symbol meaning
Ntesie maternasie
A symbol of knowledge and wisdom

The Legend of
Queen Abraha Pokou:

An Introduction

by Kofi Anyidoho

The legend of Abraha Pokou, Queen of the Baoule people, was told to me for the first time when I was about ten years old. I remember how the story of this woman, who sacrificed her only son to save her people, caught my imagination....
Pokou grew in me. I gave her a face, a life, feelings....
Pokou appeared again, in other guises, at other times, as if the legend could be told an infinite number of ways. I revisited it again and again in an effort to resolve the enigma of this woman; this mother who threw her infant into the Comoé river.

Véronique Tadjo

In oral tradition, a good tale, especially a tale worth the name of *legend*, takes on a new life with each narration, each performance. In the mouth of each creative raconteur, the legend comes to life again and again as it is re-enacted in its proper historical context but with long shadows over the present. An old but still relevant definition of legend was offered by Jacob Grimm, comparing it to the fairy-tale:

> The fairy-tale (Marchen) is with good reason distinguished from the legend, though by turns they play into one another. Looser, less fettered than legend, the fairy-tale lacks the local habitation, which hampers the legend, but makes it the more homelike. The fairy-tale flies, the legend walks, knocks at your door; the one can draw freely out of the fullness of poetry, the other has almost the authority of history. As the fairy-tale stands related to the legend, so does legend to history, and (we may add) so does history to real life.[1]

As with all borrowed definitions, especially those borrowed from other contexts or cultures, one could observe some gaps between Grimm's otherwise elegant details and the material we would find in most African contexts. For one thing, for every occurrence of *fairy-tale*, we may have to substitute *folktale*. But even for the original Grimm definition, the distinctions between the two genres must be understood to be relative rather than absolute.

In the light of the above definition, probably the most delightful surprise about Véronique Tadjo's *Queen Pokou: Concerto for a Sacrifice*, is that it has both "the fullness of poetry" and "almost the authority of history." Indeed, it is understandable that, for Amy Baram Reid, who translated the text into English from the original French version, one of her greatest challenges was how to convey the poetic essence of the

---

1   Jacob Grimm, in the Preface to the 2nd edition of his *Deutsche Mythologie* (1844), cited in Linda Degh, "Folk Narrative." In *Folklore and Folklife*: An Introduction, ed. Richard M. Dorson. University of Chicago Press, 1972, p. 72.

original. Tadjo's generous advice to her, "not only to find *le mot juste*, but to develop (her) own register for the work's poetry," must have played a key role in ensuring that the remarkable impact of this work is retained even in translation.

Probably the most important factor that enhances the poetic depth, complexity and ambiguity of this text is Tadjo's presentation of multiple versions of the legend of Queen Abraha Pokou. It is important to note that these multiple versions are not strung together in a simple serial order. There is often embedding of one version within another. Often, a version is unexpectedly truncated or interrupted at a dramatic, climactic moment, with yet another hypothetical or imagined version, or with a series of queries and intrusions of the authorial voice, urging the reader not to surrender to the enchanting power of the brutal but elusive narrative. Some versions are sparse in narrative detail, leaving significant gaps for the reader's imagination. Others are packed with bold and often shocking details.

The first, complete version of Abraha Pokou's historic escape from her ancestral royal palace and her legendary act of ultimate sacrifice, is told in the opening segment of the text, titled "The Time of Legend." Significantly, this version is told with considerable narrative detail, with hardly any digressions, except references to the persistent menace of the royal army that is closing in on Princess Pokou and her devoted followers. In this version, Pokou offers the sacrifice with almost no hesitation, almost as if it was the most logical, most natural thing to do:

> The diviner vented his rage on the people gathered along the shore: "The river requires a much greater sacrifice than all of your little trinkets! He demands an unparalleled sacrifice. That of a pure soul. By this I mean, the body of an infant."

> A servant's son was brought forth, but the old man pushed him away, saying: "What is needed is the body of a noble child."

No princess was willing to offer up her child.

Pokou took her own little son, lifted him up over her head and threw him into the waters of the river.

The ground began to tremble. Lightning bolts split the air. A gigantic, ancient tree crashed down before them. Its enormous roots lay on one shore, and its thick foliage lay on the other. Its trunk formed a natural bridge.

The people passed easily over the river.

As soon as the last man had set foot on the land of freedom, a deafening noise was again heard. The great tree broke in two and sank slowly into the water.

The king's army soon appeared on the deserted shore. On the other side of the river, Pokou's supporters watched in safety as the soldiers brandished their swords, swearing and stamping in frustration at the barrier formed by the water. (16)

Abraha Pokou's brief and repeated cry of agony that follows the child's drowning – "*Ba-ou-li*: the child is dead!" – is quickly brought to an end with a formal proclamation declaring Pokou as queen and the further proclamation to rename her people the *Baoule*, "in honour of (her) sacrifice." Perhaps this is the "official" version of the legend, the one that is supposed to anchor the Baoule people to their new home even as it links them to their ancestral Asante royal origins with an umbilical cord filled with blood and poisoned memories. It is a version of the legend that could be evoked again and again to provide a sense of pride and historical legitimacy to the Baoule people and their legendary queen.

Princess Pokou's preparedness to sacrifice her only son may have been narrated as though it were most logical, even natural. But the event that immediately follows, with the great ancient tree and the river, would seem to be anything but natural. Yet, in the true tradition of legend, even this event would be accepted as credible, in fact believable. Many definitions of legend identify *belief* as probably the most stable element, even in the face of objectively improbable occurrences. We are reminded of the observations of two leading theorists of oral narratives, Friedrich Ranke and Carl C. von Sydow, "that the story of the legend does not contain objective truth and that, nevertheless, the narrator and his audience believe it to be true."[2]

The legend of Abraha Pokou seems to have enjoyed a similar reception among the Baoule people of Côte d'Ivoire. It is indeed popular and credible enough to have been told again and again, so that Véronique Tadjo could hear it aged ten, hear it later again and again, even read it in her high school *history* text book. It is claimed that "President Félix Houphouët-Boigny, who had led the country since its independence from France in 1960, a member of the Baoule nobility, had previously drawn on the story of Abraha Pokou's sacrifice in order to bolster his own authority."[3] Hermann F. Camara, Ivorian doctoral student currently in the English Department at the University of Ghana, was emphatic in his statement to me that the legend of Abraha Pokou is indeed very popular among the Baoule people in Côte d'Ivoire. He recalled that a number of writers have taken it up in their work, citing playwright Zegoua Gbessi Nokan (Charles Nokan) and his earlier recreation of the legendary queen's story in his play *Abraha Pokou ou Une Grande Africaine suivi de La Voix grave d'Ophimoi (1970).*

It is obvious then, that Véronique Tadjo is not the first major Ivorian writer to be attracted to the legend of Queen Pokou. But it is also clear that she has used her considerable gifts and skills to endow the old legend with such unforgettable new life that the original version of her work, *Reine Pokou: Concerto pour*

---

2   Linda Degh & Andrew Vazsonyi, "Legend and Belief," in *Folkore Genres*, ed. Dan Ben-Amos. Austin & London: University of Texas Press, 1976, p. 64.

3   See translator Amy Baram Reid's essay at the end of this book, "Véronique Tadjo: Writing across literary, geographic, and linguistic borders," p. 64.

un sacrifice, received *Le Grand Prix littéraire d'Afrique Noire* when it was released in 2005. It is a work destined to bring Tadjo as much critical acclaim as *L'Ombre d'Imana: Voyages jusqu'au bout du Rwanda* (2000) [translated as *The Shadow of Imana: Travels in the Heart of Rwanda*, by Véronique Wakerley, (Heinemann, 2002)].

Elsewhere, I have suggested that an African "writer's ability to adopt and adapt oral styles and techniques is a far more significant case of creative continuity than the incorporation of fragments of folklore into written literature."[4] In the first complete version of the legend as told in "The Time of Legend," the opening segment of her work, Tadjo may have kept as close to the essentials of the legend as she had heard it. But even here, her unique style and authorial voice is unmistakable, as may be noticed, for example, in the terse, poetic narration of the exodus: "The fugitives plunged ever deeper into the forest, the realm of spirits impatient with mankind. The ground was damp, covered with a thick layer of dark soil where snakes lay in wait." (12)

Remarkable as this narrative voice is, it lacks the detailed, frightening flourish of the same event as recounted in a later version of the legend, in the second section titled "The Time of Questioning:"

> Legend says that Pokou's exodus was slow and exhausting. The trees in the forest turned into monstrous spirits who grabbed the legs of those who were fleeing and strangled the most vulnerable with their vines. From all sides, beasts came out of their lairs to circle around them, smelling their fear and the blood of the wounded, which left red stains on the rich soil of the forest. Hyenas tracked them. Elephants, their trunks held high and their ears

---

4   Kofi Anyidoho, "Kofi Awoonor and the Ewe Tradition of Songs of Abuse (*Halo*)." In *Toward Defining the African Aesthetic*. Ed. Lemuel Johnson et al. Washington DC: Three Continents Press (1982): 17-29. Reprinted in *Ghanaian Literatures*. Ed. Richard K. Priebe. New York: Greenwood Press (1988): 87-102.

waving like fans, made the ground tremble beneath their weight. On the carpet of dead leaves, snakes followed noiselessly, their scales shining with deadly glimmers. Monkeys snickered.

The air was damp, the atmosphere suffocating. The men's brows burned; their shoulders dripped with sweat. The children shivered with malarial fevers. The women's backs were broken by suffering. Everything combined to bring about their loss. They were a vanquished people fleeing a fratricidal war that nothing could stop. (23)

The deliberate piling of detail upon detail, driven home for the reader by nouns, verbs and adjectives that underscore the dangers and the suffering, sets apart this version and others to follow from the earlier version which, as we have suggested, probably comes closest to an "official" version of the legend, one that we are likely to encounter in contexts of formal political or politicized discourse. The earlier version closes on a celebrative, even if muted, note. The new one is inserted into a series of questions, questions not only about the veracity of the legend, but also about its ultimate purpose, and above all, its cost to Abraha Pokou's basic human instincts and aspirations. The questioning extends even to the gods themselves:

To what divinity did they make such a sacrifice?
To whom did they offer up the death of a child?
And just where were Africa's forgiving gods? (22)

Against such troubling questions, recitations of Abraha Pokou's royal attributes begin to sound somewhat shallow, indeed hollow. At final reckoning, the lure of power and royal glory is overwhelmed by deeper human instincts of a loving mother:

But now that the waters had closed upon the child, Abraha Pokou herself fell to her knees. She wanted to go no further. She cried out: "No Kingdom is worth the sacrifice of a child!" She wept. Finally, she threw herself on the ground and rolled from side to side, holding her head in her hands. All of a sudden she tore off her wrapper, revealing her blinding nudity. She tore at her hair, scratched her skin. Blood flowed, mixing with sweat and dust. (28)

It is important to pay close attention to the complexity of Abraha Pokou's character as presented in these multiple versions of the legend. She is at once an ideal woman and a demonic ruler driven by a constant lust for power and royal glory; a woman gifted with remarkable intelligence and yet sometimes afflicted with irrational, even suicidal and murderous instincts. Often tender, loving and gracious, she is also "a woman of steel" capable of putting all humaneness on hold.

These contradictory tendencies in Abraha Pokou's characterization, taken together with the multiple versions of the legend, may be seen as a demonstration of what translator Amy Reid identifies as a "recurrent motif" in Véronique Tadjo's life and work: border-crossing. "She consistently seeks to challenge both accepted generic boundaries and accepted truths in her artistic work." In keeping with this motif, Reid suggests that we see "*Queen Pokou,* (as) a work that not only challenges the arbitrary borders between literary genres but, more significantly, invites readers to reconsider the ethical and aesthetic implications of the stories and histories we take for granted."[5] The concern with education in "ethical and aesthetic" values noted here is indeed a hallmark of Tadjo's work, and it coincides with an important dimension of folk legend, as observed by various scholars:

---

5   See page 61.

> The reason for telling a legend is basically not to entertain but to educate people, to inform them about an important fact, to arm them against danger within their own cultural environment... [U]nderstanding of the legend is possible if one views it through the general living conditions, belief, and ideology of a culture.[6]

The last point in the above quotation draws our attention to the circumstances that appear to have inspired, perhaps compelled Tadjo to undertake this remarkable revival of the Legend of Queen Abraha Pokou – the political and social upheavals that tore Côte d'Ivoire apart and plunged the country into a civil war from which it is, even now, still struggling to recover. As Tadjo herself states in her prelude, the otherwise beautiful and inspiring legend of this Amazon she first encountered as a child, returned to her decades later when:

> Violence and war engulfed our lives, making the future seem uncertain. Then Pokou appeared to me in a more sinister light: as a queen thirsting for power; listening to the whispers of secret voices; ready to do anything to ascend to the throne.
> Pokou appeared again, in other guises, at other times, as if the legend could be told an infinite number of ways. (1)

Folk narrative scholars remind us that often the legend "invites symbolic interpretation... But in the interpretation of special traits opinions can differ, and arbitrary judgment easily slips in."[7] Readers of this legend with no particular stakes in the internecine war that has overwhelmed Côte d'Ivoire, are likely

---

6   Linda Degh, "Folk Narrative." In *Folklore and Folklife*: An Introduction, ed. Richard M. Dorson. University of Chicago Press, 1972, p. 73.

7   Max Luthi, "Aspects of the Marchen and the Legend." In *Folkore Genres*, ed. Dan Ben-Amos. Austin & London: University of Texas Press, 1976, p. 24.

to conclude that probably the most significant, perhaps intended, lesson of Véronique Tadjo's remarkable invocation of Queen Abraha Pokou's great sacrifice, is the reminder that if only we could go back a little and take in the broad sweep of our collective histories, we should soon discover that destructive, suicidal power struggles over citizenship rights in African nation states often overlook the historical truth that most, perhaps all of us may have originated somewhere outside the current boundaries of our so called modern nations. This truth, however, is not necessarily or always evident. It is in constant danger of being subverted, either through basic ignorance or forgetfulness, or through deliberate distortion, sometimes perpetrated by malicious elders seeking political capital, who would strip the legend of its "magical power" and pass it down cold and hollow in the name of education, allowing it to sink into the minds of school children who recite the tragic story of this mother without understanding the meaning of her sacrifice.

> Children in the midst of war. Tomorrow, child-soldiers.
> Thus, in the deepest recesses of our unconsciousness, and deprived of its sap, the myth follows its own path.
> What we see when we dare to take a closer look at ourselves, when we dare to stare into the magma of our becoming, is truly frightful. (54–5)

To help us contemplate the tragic consequences of our failure to fully appreciate the true meaning of Abraha Pokou's sacrifice, Tadjo gives us one imagined version of the legend, "The Atlantic Passage," in which Pokou refuses "to give her only son as an offering to the spirit of the river." In many ways, it is the version in which she and her people suffer the greatest and ultimate tragedy. Despite the bravery of her warriors and the women, and their victory in the initial combat, the defeated but relentless and ruthless royal army returns in a surprise attack which ends in the massacre of many a brave warrior and the capture of the survivors, including Pokou and her royal son, all of whom are sold into the cargo train of the Trans-Atlantic Slave Trade. The agony of their transition from the point of capture and humiliation, through dungeons of the slave fort, across the Middle Passage and onto the plantations of sorrow in the so-called New World, is recounted in a narrative style made poignant with deliberate economy of detail, leaving deep gaps too painful for the reader's imagination to contemplate:

> The ship was a black ghost on the mourning sea; a silhouette rocking impatiently, performing a macabre and revolting dance.
> The slaves, standing naked beneath the strangers' gaze, knew that their past had disappeared. The sea surrounded them. Their homeland retreated into the distance.
> In the holds, packed in tightly, body against body, tossed about by the waves, they crashed into the dank walls. Salt burned their wounds. Excrement rotted away at their flesh. Unbreathable stench. Vomit. The rats celebrated their good fortune.
> Oh! The vastness of the sea!
> Suddenly hauled out into the light on the bridge, the slaves were blinded by the blue of a sky indifferent to their fate. Sometimes a long wail announced the plunge of a man determined to stop his journey there and then. The sharks could begin their feast.
> Nightfall. Women dragged from the holds, their thighs forced open, the insides of their bodies pierced by male members sowing the seeds of future disgrace. (36)

In refusing to sacrifice her only son for the survival and safety of her people, Abraha Pokou may have acted rationally, maybe even naturally, as a mother. In the end, however, she discovers that she has "saved" her one son only to later endure the double agony of an even more gruesome sacrifice of two sons on the slave plantation: "Abraha Pokou's two sons were captured and hanged, their bodies dragged through the dust of the neighbouring fields." (39)

In a remarkable use of contrast as a technique for deepening narrative impact, Tadjo arranges the various versions of this legend in such order that probably the most painful version is preceded by a version that is probably the most delightful in the entire text, at least for Queen Pokou and the reader, though it leaves her followers in deep and extended agony. In this version, as in that of "The Atlantic Passage," the dominant symbol is water.

We watch Pokou dive into the turbulent river, swimming against the powerful currents all the way to where the river empties itself into the open seas, still searching for her love-child now turned ocean-child. We follow Pokou into a wondrous world of rolling waves that:

> sang her praises, louder than the talking drums, louder than the voices of the people lifted in unison... Magnificent grottos formed a palace of musical caverns. On the festive horizon, the sun laid its bed alongside the queen. (29)

And can we blame Pokou for forgetting about her people, left stranded and helpless on the shore, waiting in vain for her return? She surrenders herself completely to the luxury and the fabulous poetry of this new world, where she herself is now half-fish, half-human, mammy water – mythical woman of the sea whose blinding beauty strikes those she encounters like a thunderbolt, making them numb to all reality around them. Her joy multiplies as she finds her love-child, ocean-child around her. He too has found ultimate peace, here in this liquid world where he "would remain pure, free of all taint, protected from the wounds men endlessly inflict upon each other; from the venom that poisons their lives; from the evil words that disfigure them... the guest of the gods... a traveller caught between two worlds." (30–2)

In this particular version of the legend, Tadjo's multiple gifts as storyteller, poet, and painter, combine to endow her narration with rare power and beauty: delicate brush strokes of the painter combine with the poet's abiding sense of metaphor to transform the storyteller's voice into waves of pure pleasure that sweep the reader's imagination along. For as long as the intensity of this pure artistic delight lasts, we as readers feel blessed with a feeling of relief from the agonies still awaiting Queen Pokou and her followers as they pick their way blindly towards a future filled with unknown dangers. It is the memory of this world of wonder and of fulfillment that makes the Atlantic Passage episode on slavery so unimaginably painful.

If the text were to end here, on a note of misery, the final import of Tadjo's tale would have been mournful indeed. Instead, she chooses to offer us the gift of a series of rapidly narrated episodes that alternate between despair and hope, humiliation and victory, towards a final episode that comes closest to that of the magnificent poetry of the ocean paradise. In this final episode, "The Time of the Bird-Child," we witness the resurrection of Queen Pokou's ill-fated child into a powerful symbol of liberty and hope, for a society at the mercy of men of malicious and poisonous intent, seen here in the image of the elusive black snake from which the Bird-Child delivers his people at the very end:

> The snake twists, trying to escape; he hisses and spits out his venom, but he is bolted to the ground, powerless.
> And the bird-child laughs, lifting his arms up to the sky. (60)

The last laugh, surely, must be reserved for those who have known too much misery for too long. And we are moved to join the Bird-Child in this moment of triumph blessed with a final gesture in honour of liberty. Maybe we are merely dreaming, along with Tadjo the poet-painter-storyteller, choreographer of our new dance of peace and love. But it is a beautiful dream, a dream worth sharing with our people, however unwilling, however unprepared they might seem.

Personally, I must count myself blessed with the privilege of having been asked by the Publisher, Nana Ayebia Clarke, to take up the challenge of writing the Introduction to Amy Baram Reid's beautiful translation of Véronique Tadjo's powerful story, a story on which we cannot easily put one generic label. I downloaded the manuscript in the midst of a day filled with multiple tasks. Something about the title caught my attention and compelled me to take a brief first look. Somehow, the legend took instant control of my attention, dragging me through the countless agonies and occasional triumphs of Abraha Pokou and her followers. I have no doubt that countless other readers will share my excitement over this great story. But there is one thing they may not share with me: my shock and frustration in trying to trace the legend back to its ancestral origins.

As I settled down after other readings to begin work on the Introduction, it occurred to me that given the power and popularity of this legend among the Baoule, it surely must have left bold footprints in Asante oral memory and historical records. I was naïve enough to believe that the first student of Asante history I speak to would recall with ease a version, at least a fragment of the Queen Abraha Pokou legend. Maybe I have not consulted widely enough. Perhaps there are various versions scattered and somewhat buried in faded memories and tattered archival records, waiting to be unveiled. So far, however, I have spoken to a number of colleagues, all of them professional historians, some of them specialists on Akan or even Asante history, among them Professors Robert Addo-Fenning and Kofi Darkwah and Drs. Kofi Baku and Akosua

Perbi. Everyone of them is excited about the implications of the little fragment of the legend I am able to share with them. Everyone of them can think of someone who is likely to know something about the legend. So far, however, only Professor Darkwah remembers having encountered a brief reference to it in oral tradition.

I have a bit of homework waiting to be done. I have been referred to a number of sources that *probably* might have something to say about Abraha Pokou. These sources include collections of Asante oral history done by the late Joseph Agyemang-Duah and a recently completed graduate thesis by Joseph Kwadwo Agyemang, with a very intriguing title: *The People the Boundary Could Not Divide: Gyamang of Ghana & Côte d'Ivoire in Historical Perspective (1890–1960)*. Perhaps there is information in these and/or other sources to confirm that indeed Queen Abraha Pokou is still part of Asante active memory. Until such confirmation comes, however, I am led to speculate on a rather sad and troubling possibility.

Could it be that the legend of Queen Abraha Pokou has been expunged from official Asante historical memory? This magnificent story of a heroic woman of royal pedigree, who rises against and above division and succession struggle and against overwhelming odds succeeds in establishing a new Queendom far away from her place of royal ancestry, may be a source of great pride and inspiration to the Baoule people of Côte d'Ivoire. But to the ruling elite of their royal ancestral home in Ghana, it must be a story that carries a huge burden of embarrassment and guilt, maybe even pain. We are told of an old custom among the Asante and other kingdoms or empires, of enacting an oath that officially imposes a prohibition on all references to an extremely unpleasant event that has the capacity to embarrass, even destabilize the harmony of constituted royal authority. Among the Asante, this royal fiat is known as *Ntam Kesea*, the Great Oath. Tadjo leaves us in no doubt about the insecurity and ruthlessness of the elderly uncle "and an astute manipulator" who usurps the Golden Stool:

> Surrounded by his trusted advisors, the new monarch spent the night after his ascension to the throne awake, elaborating a plan that would secure his authority once and for all. Before the cock had crowed, his decision was made. There could not be two kings; Dakon would have to be eliminated.
> He had him strangled as he slept. (13)

Given how far he was prepared to go to ensure his survival on the stool, it is conceivable that having missed the chance to physically eliminate Princess Pokou and her son, rightful heir to the stool, it would not have been difficult for the unnamed usurper king to prohibit all references to Princess Pokou and her lineage. At any rate, any references to her would most certainly cast her as a dangerous rebel rather than a heroic figure. It is in this subversion of an otherwise beautiful legend that we find the grave danger, that 'truly frightful magma of our becoming' Véronique Tadjo warns us against.

And the caution is not just for her Ivorian people. It has equal relevance for all of Africa, all of humanity. In Ghana, for instance, we know of similar other legends. There is that of the Mossi, the 12th century Legend of Yennenga, in which a princess from the Dagomba royal house leads an exodus disguised as a male warrior riding on an old stallion, eventually founding a new Mossi Queendom in what is now known as Burkina Faso. It so happens that Yennenga's exodus was also faced with the obstacle of a river in flood. And if we were to pursue the full implications of our speculation, should we not be reflecting also on the significance, even as coincidence, of the fact that in each of these two historically based legends, the exodus is led by a female member of the royal house? One thing is certain, that while the men are busy trying to bring ruin to the royal house and unleash chaos on society as a whole, there is often at least one woman who rises to the challenge of conceiving a new life for her people, even if it means relocating to a new and more fertile soil.

In the end, our individual and collective lives are defined by the stories we choose or are taught to tell to ourselves about ourselves and about other people with whom we share the world, our world. And it is not just what the stories say or are intended to imply, but what we choose to make of them. Stories do not tell just one thing to all people or even to the same people every time they are told. What the stories mean to us depends to a large extent on our human capacity to embrace values or the truth encoded in them, however unpleasant. And there is never just one story, either. Nor only one truth. No matter how useful we find a particular story at a particular time in our lives, we must acknowledge the possible existence of other stories, each with its own implied truth, some of which may compete with our favourite story, and the truth as we conceive it. We must acknowledge that each story, each truth, including our favourite one, has the potential to make or unmake our world.

Accra, Ghana.
August 22, 2009.

Prelude

*T*he legend of Abraha Pokou, Queen of the Baoule people, was told to me for the first time when I was about ten years old. I remember how the story of this woman, who sacrificed her only son to save her people, caught my imagination – the imagination of a young girl living in Abidjan. I saw Pokou as a sort of Black Madonna.

Later, when I was in high school, I came upon the story of the sacrifice again, this time in my history book. In the chapter on the Ashanti Kingdom of the eighteenth century, a little aside explained that the exodus of the queen and her followers, after a battle over succession, had led to the founding of the Baoule Kingdom. Abraha Pokou took on the stature of an historic figure; an Amazon leading her people to freedom.

Pokou grew in me. I gave her a face, a life, feelings.

Several decades later, violence and war engulfed our lives, making the future seem uncertain. Then Pokou appeared to me in a more sinister light: as a queen thirsting for power; listening to the whispers of secret voices; ready to do anything to ascend to the throne.

Pokou appeared again, in other guises, at other times, as if the legend could be told an infinite number of ways. I revisited it again and again in an effort to resolve the enigma of this woman; this mother who threw her infant into the Comoé river.

I

The Time of Legend

In the time of the powerful Ashanti Kingdom, on a day when the winds of the Harmattan blew, Abraha Pokou was born in the capital, Kumasi. The air was dry, heavy with dust, and the palace was swallowed up in the haze. She was the niece of the great king, Osei Tutu, whose invincible army had as its emblem locusts – those long-legged insects that attack by the thousands, all at once, destroying everything in their path.

A few months after her birth, the baby girl was laid down to rest on a mat in the family courtyard, while her mother was cooking and everyone went about their daily activities. As she slept peacefully in the shade of a beautiful, hundred-year-old mango tree, a sudden great gust of wind sent the dust swirling up in the air. This woke the child up and made her cry. Surprised, her mother gathered her in her arms and sought shelter in the living quarters. But when she glanced down at her daughter, she was horrified to see that her hair had grown like weeds, and that it was now as thick and bushy as a field of wild corn.

Their hearts beating wildly, Pokou's parents took her to one of the best diviners in the Kingdom. He examined the baby with the greatest care. He ran his fingers through her thick hair again and again. Anguish filtered into the silence.

Finally, after declaring that a great destiny awaited her, the old man gave the little girl back to her parents. Yes, she would distinguish herself from the rest – because of her royal blood, of course – but mostly because she had been chosen by the spirits of the clan. Her surprising head of hair was proof of it.

But the man added: I see suffering and glory. Much suffering in glory.

The princess grew up, well protected and cherished by all.

She was free to gambol through the clearings, to bathe in the rivers, and to use a sling-shot to hunt lizards or little palm rats. She didn't hesitate to challenge the boys to a race, whether on foot or through the water.

She also joined in the games of the other little girls her age, who stayed close to their mothers in the royal courtyard.

The years passed and the little girl grew tall and slender, her chest filled out. Soon she would begin to prepare for her future role as wife and mother. She was often given care of an infant, which she carried strapped onto her back.

Abraha Pokou's grandmother, the venerable elder, took it upon herself to teach her the family genealogy and all the great deeds of her forebears. Each time they met, she reminded her pupil that the Golden Stool had come down from the sky and lighted on the knees of her uncle, Osei Tutu, singling him out as a divine monarch:

"Osei Tutu reigns over the whole Kingdom. He reigns over the trees, the animals and the men. We are all at his orders. He can walk on our heads, if he so wishes, with the same ease as we walk on the ground."

> *If the King is well*
> *Prosperity will rule.*
> *If the King dances,*
> *Happiness will fill all hearts.*
> *If the King ceases to eat,*
> *Famine will ensue.*
> *If the King touches his bare foot to the ground,*
> *A catastrophe will occur.*
> *If thunderbolts crash above his head,*
> *That means war is looming,*
> *And it will be horrific.*

However, the elder did not fail to caution her young pupil: "My child, pay close attention to the world around you at nightfall. Hear how it sighs after the excesses of the sun. Darkness brings relief. The golden light tantalises our eyes. Do not ever let yourself be carried away by greed."

Pokou listened respectfully, but took an excessive pleasure in asking questions about all sorts of things. Sometimes, worn out by the girl's curiosity, the old woman reminded her of the strictures attached to such knowledge: "What I am about to tell you, I am telling your ears and not your mouth! Understand me well, but do not pass on my words carelessly. If you know how to be patient, I will reveal many secrets to you. They will come one by one, because no one says everything the same day."

Recognised for her intelligence as much as for her beauty, Pokou walked with her head held high.

The young girl understood that the time for her to marry was not far off when she saw that her former playmates had suddenly become men. Some had already been introduced into her family circle. Although she would have preferred not to think about it, Pokou knew that she needed to make her wishes known quickly, before a decision was made for her. The physical and moral qualities of her intended mattered more than his social standing. If he was handsome, her child would be too. If he was intelligent, her child would be too.

With the king's permission and her grandmother's approval, Abraha Pokou was united with the one who had long been her best friend.

The first year of marriage was a time of happiness. The second, much less so, for the young wife's belly failed to grow round. It seemed that no child wished to leave the realm of shadows to settle there. The third year was poisoned by endless quarrels: Pokou was sterile. No, her husband was dry. Pokou had angered the spirits. No, her husband simply did not deserve to share the bed of a princess.

Because of her royal blood, Pokou could have had her

husband sentenced to death, had she so desired. She was satisfied just to repudiate him.

But it was too late, wicked tongues were already unleashed: "A childless woman is like a bitter herb mixed into a sauce: it makes it inedible."

Meanwhile, at that very time, a great tragedy befell the Ashanti people.

Osei Tutu, the Beloved Monarch, the Revered King, the Guardian of the Golden Stool, a man perfect in both body and soul, was treacherously killed in an ambush.

His death, as violent as it was unexpected, plunged the Ashanti Kingdom into a period of darkness. Daily activities stopped to make way for mourning and the precise fulfillment of the funeral rites.

Several months passed before life resumed its flow.

When Opokou Waré, Pokou's brother and Osei Tutu's chosen heir, sat upon the Golden Throne, the young woman's life changed radically. From then on she had full access to the corridors of power, and was able to observe the art of ruling. This she did with great interest.

In the years that followed, Pokou had other husbands. She made regular sacrifices to the gods and also beseeched the ancestors to intercede on her behalf:

Oh providential Fathers
You have given children
To the other women of the Kingdom.
But me you have ignored.
The healers and the marabouts
Have failed me.
Now, I am asking you,
And you alone:
Give me a child.

Her prayers grew more and more insistent as rumours took shape and swelled: what if there were evil forces swirling around her? What if the barrenness of her womb was proof of witchcraft?

Once the target of taunts, Pokou now inspired fear.

Breaking the circle of life. What greater curse could there be for a woman?

One day Opokou Waré and his entire army set out to put down a rebellion in a distant province. A vassal chief, who refused to continue paying the heavy tribute that the king had imposed upon him, took advantage of his absence to move on the royal city, spreading terror and devastation along his path.

News of the imminent danger reached the palace.

Who was going to defend Kumasi?

A war council was called to organise the resistance. Pokou sat unnoticed in a corner and listened to what the dignitaries had to say. Their words gave voice to the panic felt by all. The queen mother, who had assumed power in the absence of her son, suggested that the few weapons that remained hidden away be distributed to the slaves and to the women and children who felt able to fight.

Hearing that, Pokou quickly stood up and asked permission to make another suggestion. One notable wanted to stop her from doing so, but the queen mother commanded that she be allowed to speak.

Here is what the princess said: "We cannot ask innocent women and children who have never fought to take up arms. They will not be able to stand up to an army of evil-doers."

"Get to the point. Just what are you suggesting?" snapped one high dignitary, angrily.

"Evacuate the city immediately and, once you've securely hidden away the Golden Stool and the symbols of the monarchy, take cover yourselves in the forests that surround the city. But leave the royal coffers where they are: that's what they are coming for."

"Abandon the treasure!?" exclaimed one man with a shaved head. "That would be the end of the Kingdom!"

"Would you prefer to save your life or go to your death surrounded by riches?" retorted Pokou with a certain insolence. Without waiting for an answer, she sat down again.

A long rumble of disapproval ran through the assembly. And yet, when the council resumed its deliberations, the notables quickly came to the conclusion that Pokou's plan should be adopted and put into action without delay.

So it came as a great surprise when, as everyone was about to depart, Pokou announced that she would not leave the palace. She had decided to stay with those who were too weak to make the journey. No one could dissuade her.

Frustrated to have invaded an abandoned palace, the enemy forces profaned the king's residence. Moving from room to room, they ransacked the palace, and took whatever they pleased – ornaments, jewels, valuable wrappers, ivory statues...

When they found the stores of alcohol and food, they drank and ate like gluttons. As predicted, the coffers of the royal treasury were emptied.

As they were about to leave the palace, the pillagers discovered the room where Pokou and her companions were hiding. They would have killed them on the spot if someone hadn't recognised the king's sister. All too happy to take hostage a member of the royal family's inner circle, they left behind the others, scorning their pitiful infirmities.

When they returned to Kumasi, Opokou Waré and his warriors found the city pillaged and the palace in ruins. After hearing accounts of the attack and the abduction of his sister, the king set off in pursuit.

Very quickly they caught up with the drunken captors, whose flight had been slowed considerably by the excessive weight of their booty. Unaware of the looming danger, they were laughing loudly, congratulating themselves on the humiliation they had just inflicted on the great monarch. The Ashanti warriors fell upon them mercilessly. They freed Pokou and took back the royal treasures.

The leader of the insurgents was beheaded, and his head brought back to Kumasi, where it was exposed on a pike in front of the palace walls. As for the prisoners, they were led through the town, naked and bound at the wrists, while the people jeered and pelted them with stones. Locked up in the storehouses, they would later be sold to slave traders.

A lavish greeting awaited Pokou in the capital. She was covered with honours and rewards: three sacks of gold nuggets, fifteen slaves and a sacred throne, one of the Kingdom's highest distinctions.

Her courage was publicly acknowledged.

Following this event, the king began to consult regularly with his sister. They would talk privately about daily affairs, future military campaigns, and of the trade in gold, kola nuts, and slaves. Pokou would say to him:

"Be careful. The whites who have settled on the coast are interested only in the wealth from your gold mines and the slaves you can provide them. They are insatiable. Soon you will need to send your men to search in places farther and farther away. Be careful: today their long guns make you powerful, but tomorrow they may be turned against you."

One day, with no warning at all, a man asked for Pokou's hand in marriage. An officer in the royal army, it was he who had freed her following her abduction. She welcomed this marriage as a gift from the gods.

Only a few months after their union, Abraha Pokou was amazed to discover that she was expecting a child.

The birth was marked with many ceremonies.

Pokou solemnly addressed the ancestors: "Here is the son you have given me. I thank you for hearing my prayers. In return, I promise he will honour you his whole life!"

Turning to face the crowd, the oracle proclaimed in a booming voice: "You who are gathered here, salute this child! Thanks to him, a powerful Kingdom will rise."

Pokou had never been happier. What more could she want? She had everything. Fate had finally smiled upon her. The days passed in the sweet flowering of maternal love. She forgot all about politics and intrigue.

But History did not stop its advance. During a military campaign, Opokou Waré fell ill. Gravely ill. He was brought back on a litter, after a march of several days. The palace healers gave him bitter potions to drink; they covered him in poultices, and made him breathe in the smoke from smouldering blends of leaves and bark. Throughout the night, incense burned to purify the sick man's room.

The priests demanded sacrifices. The marabouts from the Great Mosque in the Islamic quarter inserted verses from the Koran into amulets which they placed around his bed.

All in vain.

Feeling that the time had come for him to join the ancestors, the King named his successor. On the advice of Pokou, his choice fell upon Dakon, their half-brother, whose faithfulness and dedication were beyond question.

Opokou Waré confided the secrets of power to Dakon. He regurgitated the royal ring which he had kept in his stomach for decades and held it out to Dakon, who swallowed it, after pledging that the new reign would always uphold with greatest respect the principles of the monarchy.

Soon after, the king, wracked by illness, gave up his life in this world. The end of his reign had come.

The queen mother whispered sacred words in the ears of her deceased son while the priests poured a mixture of water, alcohol, gold dust, and precious gems into his mouth.

"Nana," murmured the high priest, "when death claims its prey, we cannot stop it from swallowing him up."

All the provincial chiefs gathered in Kumasi to take part in funeral ceremonies worthy of such a great monarch. All across the Kingdom, the people's grief was sincere, and continued throughout the period of mourning.

Then came the time to elect a new king. Everything suggested that it would be an easy task, as the final wishes of the deceased king were usually respected.

But in fact, the council proved to be profoundly divided. One group of dignitaries opposed Dakon, feeling that Abraha Pokou would have too much influence over her half-brother and that it would be better to place power in the hands of a more experienced man. Others thought they should respect the wishes of the deceased, who knew better than anyone the qualities necessary to become a good leader.

At the end of a bitter debate that inflamed malevolent passions, Dakon was shoved aside, wholly excluded from power. An elderly uncle of the royal family, and an astute manipulator, was elected in his place.

The old man assumed his place on the Golden Stool in a hastily organised ceremony. He was not carried in triumph across the whole city, as tradition required – the situation was still far too tense in the Kingdom.

Surrounded by his trusted advisors, the new monarch spent the night after his ascension to the throne awake, elaborating a plan that would secure his authority once and for all. Before the cock had crowed, his decision was made. There could not be two kings; Dakon would have to be eliminated.

He had him strangled as he slept.

After this assassination, the life of Pokou's son was suddenly in danger. According to the laws of matriarchal lineage, he was next in line for the stool. The very presence of the child and his mother in the Kingdom constituted a threat to the king's absolute authority. Besides, the old uncle didn't really care for his niece, whom he accused of harbouring inordinate ambitions. He also felt that she was too close to the high priests.

Murders and disappearances multiplied in Kumasi. Whole sections of the city were set ablaze, their inhabitants caught and killed in broad daylight. All the members of the council who had supported Dakon disappeared. Their mutilated corpses were later found in piles of waste.

Should she flee with her child? Abandon the other members of her family, her husband and her brother's many supporters? No, Pokou refused even to consider it.

When an officer of the former royal guard came to warn her that orders had been given for her elimination and that she should flee without delay, the young woman replied: "I refuse to run away like some common thief. I am protected by my brother's spirit. With the support of the gods, I will find a solution."

But when Dakon's mother died in her arms, stabbed in the back, Pokou decided to organise the exodus of all those whose safety was threatened.

In utmost secrecy, Pokou met with a Muslim trader based in Kumasi. She was convinced he would make a good guide because he had travelled far and wide. The merchant suggested they head west. In those territories there were immense forests with splendid trees. Their foliage was so thick that there was twilight beneath them, even when the sun was at its highest overhead. The ground was fertile; very fertile. A piece of wood shoved into the earth instantly took root.

At dawn's first light, Pokou and her followers were already far away, forming a long line that weaved through the bush.

A group was sent ahead to scout out the path; they listened carefully for the slightest sound or sign of danger. They even climbed up into the trees to scan the surrounding area.

At regular intervals, the hunters blew their horns to encourage the advancing column. The fugitives plunged ever deeper into the forest, the realm of spirits impatient with mankind. The ground was damp, covered with a thick layer of dark soil where snakes lay in wait.

As they made their way they came upon several villages, which they avoided, on the advice of the advance party. The villages were still too close to Kumasi and would certainly have betrayed them. On the other hand, they welcomed lone travellers into their ranks, and hunters showed them where to find fresh water and game.

They made slow progress; their path was littered with dangers. At times they were overcome with profound despair.

After walking for several days, the column stopped. The situation was dire; they needed a plan. Pokou's husband, accompanied by a handful of dignitaries and a well-armed guard, would turn back to face the royal army. Their mission was to stall the army for as long as possible, under the pretext that Pokou and her followers had decided to give up and return to Kumasi.

The trick bore fruit. The leaders of the two sides set up camp in the middle of the forest to negotiate a settlement. There were libations, offerings, a palaver. Endless negotiations stretched out into pointless discussions.

Exasperated, the leader of the royal army finally understood that he had been tricked. Wild with rage, he had the throats of all of Pokou's representatives slit, and then raced off on the trail of the fugitives.

When Pokou's spies brought back word of this, she almost collapsed under the weight of her suffering. She began to doubt whether the exodus had been the right decision: "Are the ancestors with us or against us? Why are the spirits abandoning us, after all that we have given them?"

Among the ranks of the fugitives, it was whispered that Pokou's stubbornness was the cause of their sad fate. What was pushing her to keep moving ahead, dragging all of them along in a flight that would end in their deaths?

Pokou asked the diviner to show her which path to follow: "What do you see in the signs? Should we persevere or give ourselves up?"

"We must continue," he answered. "I see much more pain and suffering ahead, but once we have crossed the border and left Ashanti-land, your destiny as a queen will begin."

The king's army was on their heels.

But then the column was stopped in its tracks by the Comoé river, whose turbulent waters marked the edge of the Kingdom. On the far shore lay freedom. Behind them, death.

A few men tried to swim across the waters, but they were immediately carried away by the current.

The high priest went off alone to confer with the spirit of the waters.

He returned with a solemn face: "No one will be able to cross until we have made a sacrifice."

After gathering the few jewels and other precious objects they had managed to carry away with them, the fugitives threw them one by one into the river.

The offerings had no effect on the water's anger.

The diviner vented his rage on the people gathered along the shore: "The river requires a much greater sacrifice than all of your little trinkets! He demands an unparalleled sacrifice. That of a pure soul. By this I mean, the body of an infant."

A servant's son was brought forth, but the old man pushed him away, saying: "What is needed is the body of a noble child."

No princess was willing to offer up her child.

Pokou took her own little son, lifted him up over her head and threw him into the waters of the river.

The ground began to tremble. Lightning bolts split the air. A gigantic, ancient tree crashed down before them. Its enormous roots lay on one shore, and its thick foliage lay on the other. Its trunk formed a natural bridge.

The people passed easily over the river.

As soon as the last man had set foot on the land of freedom, a deafening noise was again heard. The great tree broke in two and sank slowly into the water.

The king's army soon appeared on the deserted shore. On the other side of the river, Pokou's supporters watched in safety as the soldiers brandished their swords, swearing and stamping in frustration at the barrier formed by the water.

And thus the exiled were able to set up camp in a vast green clearing.

The high priest turned toward them and said: "If we are now free, we owe it to the courage and noble spirit of an exceptional woman. Let us beseech her to become our queen."

"We beseech her to become our queen!" shouted the people as one.

But Pokou, with her head bowed down, just kept repeating, "*Ba-ou-li*: the child is dead!"

And so the elders gathered around her in a circle and declared: "Henceforth we shall call ourselves 'Baoule' – the Baoule people – in honour of your sacrifice."

II

The Time of
Questioning

Abraha Pokou: Fallen Queen

According to legend, Queen Pokou had to sacrifice her child to save her people. Sacrifice her child to save her people.

The child had to die. The woman tore out her own insides, closed her belly back up again, wiped out her maternal instincts, and hardened her heart for good. She became the queen of a great people, but a beggar of that strongest of loves.

The waters parted, it is said, after they had swallowed up the child; after they had tossed it to and fro, brutalised and devoured it; they parted so that the column of refugees could continue its exodus.

That's how the queen's exile began: an exile to the deepest part of her broken, shattered soul. She was empty, filled with the void left by the child, even as everything still reminded her of his birth: the stretch marks on her belly, grotesque welts where the skin, like a cloth pulled too tightly, had cracked. And her breasts, swollen with milk, now weighed too heavy under her regal wrapper.

She knew that she would carry this absence from that day forward and to the very end: nothing, not power, nor honours, could ever erase it.

"*Ba-ou-li*: the child is dead!"

In the mouths of future generations, Baoule became the name of the Kingdom built upon the death of a child; the child-king whose body finally rose to the surface, a ripe fruit, and burst under the weight of the water.

Or maybe those were his limbs that the men and women discovered discarded on the shore after the crocodiles and crabs had had their feast; the prince whose blood turned the waters red to save the future from certain disaster.

And the people, what did they say?

"*Ba-ou-li*: the child is dead!"

To what divinity did they make such a sacrifice?
To whom did they offer up the death of a child?
And just where were Africa's forgiving gods?

A group of men – the leaders – stood before the barrier of water that blocked their advance. They had gathered together and spoken at length with the diviner, observing the signs and trying to understand the direction destiny was taking them.

The wait was unbearable. The river's endless roar filled the tired, weary people with fear. Deep in the forest, the army, bent on revenge, was advancing rapidly toward them.

Pokou held her child in her arms. Murmuring sweet words and humming lullabies to calm the pain of such a long march, she hugged him tight.

Could it be that when they saw that princess, weaker and more fragile than the most ordinary of women, the dignitaries wanted to show the impatient and cruel gods that they, too, knew how to speak their language?

With the dull light of the morning, they went to Abraha Pokou to inform her of the river spirit's demands. She let out a long wail that rose above the treetops and spread out over the distance. The sun awoke with a start, bringing down upon them an intense heat.

And when she looked at her son, curled up in his bed of fresh grasses, she understood that she was damned. Time was fixed forever. She would remain shut away in her vast solitude, walled up for the rest of her life.

But is the story true? Did the waters of the Comoé river open up to let the faithful pass over and escape?

Did the waters really split apart as they had for Moses and the Jews?

Legend says that Pokou's exodus was slow and exhausting. The trees in the forest turned into monstrous spirits who grabbed the legs of those who were fleeing and strangled the most vulnerable with their vines. From all sides, beasts came out of their lairs to circle around them, smelling their fear and the blood of the wounded, which left red stains on the rich soil of the forest. Hyenas tracked them. Elephants, their trunks held high and their ears waving like fans, made the ground tremble beneath their weight. On the carpet of dead leaves, snakes followed noiselessly, their scales shining with deadly glimmers. Monkeys snickered.

The air was damp, the atmosphere suffocating. The men's brows burned; their shoulders dripped with sweat. The children shivered with malarial fevers. The women's backs were broken by suffering. Everything combined to bring about their loss. They were a vanquished people fleeing a fratricidal war that nothing could stop.

Did the waters really split apart to let the people pass through?

Abraha Pokou – with her black and velvety skin, her indigo eyes, and the body of a gazelle – was a beauty among the beautiful.

Abraha Pokou, Princess of Kumasi; niece of Osei Tutu, the powerful and awesome King of the Ashanti, the great conqueror, master of gold and kola;

Daughter of Nyakou Kosiamoa, sister of Opokou Waré, half-sister of Dakon;

Dakon, the ill-fated monarch who was assassinated, his Queen Mother stabbed, the royal family massacred, and his whole court destroyed;

23

Abraha Pokou, miraculously spared so that she could lead the faithful in a painful exodus;

Abraha Pokou, destined for greatness, who deserved to live out her life adorned with jewels and honours.

Alas! Now she knew the scent of death; that stench of earth and blood, of bodily fluids and rotting flesh. She had seen so many cadavers strewn on the palace floor: familiar faces disfigured by their death throes; the people she loved, destroyed. How she had sobbed, with the din of weapons and the dull thud of falling bodies ringing in her ears. Their cries, their last words ground out in the dust. Fires everywhere, burning up the night, turning bodies into coals.

In the white mourning of the day, death reached into the four corners of the Kingdom.

Abraha Pokou was forced to organise in haste the flight of the faithful, who were already exhausted and on the verge of despair.

In the desert of their defeat, they advanced in one long unbroken column, their bodies covered in ashes, their faces painted with kaolin, the white, chalky colour of mourning and suffering, their royal wrappers reduced to rags.

Abraha Pokou only survived by calling forth her memories: images of her happy childhood, when she ran free as an antelope, when she was neither girl nor boy, nor, above all, a princess.

Alas, time had proven her otherwise: she was not just a woman, but heiress to a royal line. From her womb a king would be born, successor to the Golden Stool, a gift from the gods to the Ashanti Kingdom. She was the guardian of tradition, the one chosen for an extraordinary destiny.

Abraha Pokou, mighty with the blessing of the ancestors;

Abraha Pokou, who had been solemnly presented to the sacred totems;

Abraha Pokou, who had grown into a true beauty;

Abraha Pokou, the one of superior intellect;

Abraha Pokou, the respectful, who knew how to honour the dead and to find the right words to please them;

Abraha Pokou, whose courage allowed her to hold her head high in the most difficult of times.

The child had illuminated her days, filled her dreams, and kept the spectre of a solitary death at bay. He would be there when she bid the world farewell. She would not fall back to the earth like some rotten and discarded branch from a tree. The legacy of the ancestors would not be profaned. The dynasty would carry on.

Pokou, who stood tall like a Baobab, her brow at once so proud and so humble. Pokou, the woman with a will of steel, looked at the son she held in her arms.

She thought of the man, his father, the warrior who had freed her from the anguish of the barren woman. She had loved him with a passion that seemed impossible after all the other unions that had lost their savour and withered away over the years without fruit. She still remembered the re-awakening of her body, the bliss of her senses, the honey that he made run in her veins, and the creamy milk that wet the inside of her thighs.

Abraha Pokou, the seductress, in love like a little girl as she reached the great turning-point of her womanhood!

She looked at the child-prince, the miraculous son, the love-child. Overwhelmed, her soul began to reel, spinning around in the troubled sky, and then to rebel, crashing against the tall trees of the forest and collapsing, only finally to fly up again and reach that place where no hope exists and where pain resumes its despotic reign.

So she lifted the child up toward the sky to present him to the gods. Then, offering them her greatest gift, she threw him into the troubled waters of the river.

The little body sank deeper as whirlpools wrapped all around him. Suddenly, the surface of the river grew calm, so calm it looked like a pool of oil in the reddening dawn.

From the mouth of the queen herself came the words of the legend that, for generation upon generation, would be sung by drums and retold in new words by the griots.

"*Ba-ou-li*: the child is dead!"

The people got down on their knees and chanted:

> *Abraha Pokou, oh mother sublime*
> *Your strength is our victory*
> *Your strength wipes away our fears*
> *Abraha Pokou, oh mother sublime*
> *The waves have parted*
> *To let us through.*
> *Our enemies tremble with rage*
> *While we tremble with joy*
> *Abraha Pokou, oh mother sublime*
> *You will found a powerful Kingdom!*

But is the legend true? Did the waters really part so that the fleeing people could pass through?

Why is it that women must always send their children off? Why isn't their love strong enough to stop wars and keep death at bay?

Maybe it was just another ritual sacrifice, one more example of the witchcraft so prevalent in the powerful Ashanti Kingdom: human sacrifices to calm the anger of the gods, to ask for the impossible or to ensure a good harvest.

Abraha Pokou's life had been woven of violence and tenderness; cruelty and love.

Her son was still of an age when he slept at her side, pressing his small body against hers, a hand on his mother's breast to signal his ownership. And despite her troubled sleep, his kicks and his early rising, she refused to detach herself from the boy. Filled with wonder, she delighted in caring for him.

Unconditional love, engraved in her soul, her secret fulfilment. The stars alone held the key to the future.

Hadn't oracles predicted a great destiny for the child?

Standing before the barrier of the waters, Pokou, who had found such fulfillment in motherhood, looked at her child one last time. Then she kissed his brow and threw him into the river.

She wanted to die, too, to let herself be swallowed up, to go to the end of her love and her pain. Her heart beat so hard it seemed it would burst; her soul wailed with despair that no one could hear. She – the ambitious one, Pokou of the queenly stature, the fertile, courageous one – she would have abandoned her Kingdom for even just one second more of her child's love. The power that was now within her grasp was too heavy for her shattered soul to bear.

This war was damned, a thousand times damned! How could her uncle have ordered his nephew's death? How could the soldiers have killed men who had once joined with them in ritual celebrations?

The army from Kumasi pursued them. How had a quarrel over succession resulted in such barbarity? In this long exodus across the forest, through the sweltering heat and the endless buzzing of insects?

Abraha Pokou thought back to the death of her beloved, the warrior and father of her child.

The river blocked their path, rendering all hope impossible. A river with a fatal bite, hysterical currents, waters of invincible fury: the rage of the gods that only a great sacrifice could calm.

Abraha Pokou walked to the river's edge and held up her child's body. Then she stretched out her arms and let him fall into the waters.

"*Ba-ou-li*: the child is dead!"

And the waves suddenly calmed. Hippopotami surfaced. Side by side they formed a solid bridge, a living bridge over which the people crossed, safe and sound.

When Abraha Pokou stepped onto the new land, with her heart exploding in her chest and her spirit paralysed by the irreparability of her actions, the people bowed down at her feet and cried. What the waters had swallowed would never again be returned.

The elders, the diviners, the oracles stood up. The most worthy among them spoke for all: "*Ba-ou-li*: the child is dead! From now on, we shall be called the Baoule people so that no one will ever forget that, for us, you agreed to sacrifice the flesh of your flesh."

But now that the waters had closed upon the child, Abraha Pokou herself fell to her knees. She wanted to go no further. She cried out: "No Kingdom is worth the sacrifice of a child!" She wept. Finally, she threw herself on the ground and rolled from side to side, holding her head in her hands. All of a sudden she tore off her wrapper, revealing her blinding nudity. She tore at her hair, scratched her skin. Blood flowed, mixing with sweat and dust.

Then, Abraha Pokou's muscles stiffened. She fell silent, still.

Unable to help her, the people just watched.

After a long while, she slowly got back up. Then, impelled by a great force, she ran to the river and, before anyone could hold her back, dived into the tumultuous waves.

The people knew then that they had lost their queen for the love of a child.

Abraha Pokou broke the surface of the river in an extraordinary dive. On she swam, looking for her son. When at last she saw his frail little body drifting with the current, she clasped him to her bosom and kept swimming. She reached the river's mouth, and then the high sea.

Days, months, and years passed by. She succeeded in conquering a Kingdom more beautiful than the one she had been promised: now, half woman, half fish, she is the unchallenged goddess of the underwater realm, queen of the oceans.

The belly of the sea is a vast womb.

And so her realm became that of the waters, an ever-shifting Kingdom, changing with the phases of the moon, with the wind and the heat of the sun. Warm currents, cold currents, meeting tumultuously to form a troubled zone, in permanent revolution. Waves copulating, liquid crystals, multi-faceted mirrors, treasure troves of shells and coral, translucent algae, stones polished by the ages to a warm and reassuring gleam.

Each day the rolling waves of the high seas sang her praises, louder than the talking drums, louder than the voices of the people lifted in unison.

There was no need to beat on the skin of a drum; the lapping of the waves was an enchanting refrain.

Queen or goddess – did it matter anymore what she was called? Did it matter at all how her face, her body, and her skin appeared, or how petrifying her gaze had become?

Magnificent grottos formed a palace of musical caverns. On the festive horizon, the sun laid its bed alongside the queen.

The ocean was never the same – one day turbulent, another calm as a dozing lake. There was no monotony.

She roamed over the sea beds, carried along by schools of fish, caressed by the algae. Flashes of silver, yellow, and phosphorescence.

Above the surface, the faithful mourned the disappearance of their queen and crown prince. Men paddled canoes far from the shore so that the priests could entrust their prayers to the crests of the waves.

Splendid Mother,
Why do you hide your beauty
Under the waves?
Bring peace back into our hearts.
Give us a bit of hope.
Bring back happier times
By bestowing your forgiveness upon us.

From the shore, the people anxiously observed the moving waters. The sea took on a blue-green hue and seemed to dance with light. The foam traced mysterious shapes – but of the queen, there was no sign.

Day after day, the priests returned sombre-faced from their expeditions on the sea.

And then the drums would confirm, once again, the absence of the queen.

"Not yet," said the elders. "It is too soon. She has not yet forgiven us."

A great sigh of disappointment ran through the assembled people.

Still, some men knew that the queen was not far away. Those foolish enough to wander on the beach after nightfall had seen her, met her in the moonlight.

With her caressing gaze and her voluptuous body, she flooded them with desire. She approached them gracefully, first touched and then embraced them. They stayed with her, inside her, until dawn. The warm sand became their wedding bed.

In this way she took possession of them: her eyes claimed their spirits, and her embrace, their bodies.

These men were no longer capable of love. No woman was able to slake their thirst, meet their desires, fulfill their dreams. They had lost the essence of life itself: the possibility of complete happiness.

As they slept, they let themselves be carried away by the winds of a storm, by a tornado of carnal pleasures. Their spirits were bound to the memory of a pleasure so intense that it threatened their very lives. They had broken the ultimate taboo.

They were tortured by their secret, which set them apart from the others. Mere shadows of themselves, these lovers-for-a-night withered before everyone's eyes, losing their strength and their will to live. Magnificent men with the bodies of athletes now wasted away, like fruits emptied of all flavour, of all substance.

The seductive power of the goddess was complete, limitless. There was no one who could resist her. Even the women she approached were stunned by her perfection and fell under the sway of her extraordinary beauty. Afterwards, when she had disappeared for good, her companions were lost in sorrow, overwhelmed by a boundless, inconsolable longing. These women gave up everything else to look for her. With a determined step, they hurried from one place to another until they collapsed from exhaustion. They were most often found alone, huddled naked on the ground.

Those women and men no longer belonged to the people. Suffering souls, they were crushed by the secret they bore.

As a lover her drives were as powerful as her maternal instinct: generous, destructive, haughty like the foaming waves. Only the sun could have stopped her.

The ocean-child, the son of sacrifice and love, was there beside her. After her exploits, she always returned to him.

Water is shapeless, colourless. Light does not touch it. Dark shadows have no effect upon it. Who can hold it in their hand? Who can order it to be still? The child felt happier in the water, as in the first moments of life, when still hidden in his mother's womb.

The ocean-child would remain pure, free of all taint, protected from the wounds men endlessly inflict upon each other; from the venom that poisons their lives; from the evil words that disfigure them.

She should never have allowed her son to leave the sheltering world of her womb. He should have stayed there, protected by the shell of her body and the warmth of her blood.

The child was soft, shapeless. His spine had disappeared. His translucent skin revealed a network of fluorescent red veins. His eyes were milky white, his hands and feet webbed.

He would never grow up; never again leave this aquatic universe. He did not want to dry out in the open air, to grow hard, bony, mean. He would never lose the freshness of his innocence. The fire of the sun and of men was far too intense.

He fed on plankton. No words came out of his mouth. No memories troubled his spirit. Time ebbed and flowed, and the child swam in a wondrous tranquility inspired by his fluid surroundings. He was the guest of the gods.

The child had been swallowed up by an unforeseen destiny. A messenger from beyond, he was a traveller caught between two worlds.

The Atlantic Passage

But what if Abraha Pokou had refused the sacrifice? What if, contrary to legend, the queen had refused to give her only son as an offering to the spirit of the river whose waters blocked the way of the fleeing people?

She stiffened her back, held her head high and declared in a loud and clear voice: "No, I will not sacrifice my son! I want to see him grow up. I want him to become a man. And, when the time has come, he will be the one to prepare me for burial."

The fugitives listened to her in a silence heavy with fear. Did the queen know what she was doing? Had she really weighed the consequences of her decision? Going against the will of the gods would only bring distress and calamity.

Ignoring the diviner who tried to interrupt, Pokou continued: "I refuse to throw my child into the tumultuous waters of the Comoé river. Do not ask that of me. Our warriors are brave. Together we will be able to defend ourselves against the army of our foes and their dogged hatred."

And so preparations began. First, hide the children and the elderly deep in the forest: in hollowed out tree trunks, bushes, tall grass, ferns, ravines, wherever a body could be concealed. The women were called to take up arms.

Pokou's warriors were good strategists; they organised ambushes. Some of the fighters would pretend to advance along the river while the others, better armed, would wait, ready to strike the enemy from behind. A series of surprise attacks should inflict losses heavy enough to make the enemy retreat, and give Abraha Pokou the time she needed to reach a large village several hours away. There she would negotiate protection for herself and her supporters. Her arrival had already been announced by those sent to scout the way ahead.

Everything happened according to plan. The king's army reached the river bank. In the battle that ensued, the ardour of Pokou's soldiers – men and women alike – more than made up for their enemy's superior numbers. They had expected to find a people trembling and weakened by several days marching through the forest. Caught in the trap, they were unprepared for such resistance and lost many men. Their chief was seriously wounded and they retreated in confusion, promising revenge.

"You won't escape! We'll be back to cut you into pieces— we'll massacre you!"

Pokou's faithful followers ended the suffering of the wounded, buried their dead and quickly resumed their march. Those who were hurt but who could still be transported were carried on makeshift stretchers.

At the end of the day, the column reached the large village found by the advance party. Neat rows of huts exuded an air of peace and prosperity. The villagers came out as they arrived. Abraha Pokou, holding her son in her arms, introduced herself. She was led to the home of the chief, with whom she spoke at length. He then went to consult with the village elders. A little while later, Abraha Pokou was led before the assembled crowd. Once the ritual greetings were exchanged, the chief's spokesman addressed her directly:

"War brought you here. We cannot abandon you in the forest. That would go against our traditions. We remember well that your brother, Opokou Waré, was a good monarch. So we will find room for you and your supporters in our village. You

34

will drink, eat, and sleep. When you have regained your strength, you can go on your way. We will show you the surest route around the river."

The villagers treated the new arrivals with hospitality. They settled them comfortably in their compounds, or inside their huts when they had enough room. They also helped them to care for the wounded.

A feeling of relief overcame the fugitives. There still seemed to be reason for hope. A different life, and fertile land, awaited them on the other side of the river. Their suffering had not been in vain.

The moon gleamed in its pale yellow light.

Suddenly, a stifling glow roused the sleepers from their heavy slumber. The huts were burning. Thick smoke rose right up to the sky. The villagers ran from their homes. They were met by the king's soldiers and the deafening din of their gunfire. Bullets flew in all directions.

There was nowhere to run. No room for compassion. Blood! Everywhere blood!

Charred flesh, corpses. The village was ablaze and its destruction lit up the far-corners of the surrounding darkness.

The survivors were rounded up under the great kapok tree. The villagers, led by their chief, had to promise allegiance to the victors in order to save their own lives. Standing among the prisoners, holding the child-king crying in her arms, Pokou knew all too well that a fate worse than death awaited them all.

The army from Kumasi had pursued them, refusing to give up its prey. Now they would be bound hand and foot, then sold to stony-faced men.

The general of the royal army could not contain his disdain for Pokou: "If it were up to me, I would have already cut off your head and displayed it to the whole of Kumasi! But the King ordered me not to shed a drop of your blood. You'll be sent somewhere else to rot!"

Bound in chains and abused, the captives knew that every step brought them closer to a fatal destiny. Should they have negotiated instead of fighting? Accepted that they could never stand up against the king's power? Wasn't it better to die at once than to spend the rest of their days suffering at the hands of cruel barbarians?

Soon, with their eyes reddened by suffering, they discovered the ocean – immense, violent, unfathomable. Men with skin like shrouds were there as well. They circled around the merchandise:

> *Count the teeth, squeeze the muscles.*
> *Separate the men from the women.*
> *Reject the wounded, the sick, the weak.*
> *Keep a few children.*
> *Haggle, take the goods away.*

The ship was a black ghost on the mourning sea; a silhouette rocking impatiently, performing a macabre and revolting dance.

The slaves, standing naked beneath the strangers' gaze, knew that their past had disappeared. The sea surrounded them. Their homeland retreated into the distance.

In the holds, packed in tightly, body against body, tossed about by the waves, they crashed into the dank walls. Salt burned their wounds. Excrement rotted away at their flesh. Unbreathable stench. Vomit. The rats celebrated their good fortune.

Oh! The vastness of the sea!

Suddenly hauled out into the light on the bridge, the slaves were blinded by the blue of a sky indifferent to their fate. Sometimes a long wail announced the plunge of a man determined to stop his journey there and then. The sharks could begin their feast.

Nightfall. Women dragged from the holds, their thighs forced open, the insides of their bodies pierced by male members sowing the seeds of future disgrace.

The great exile. Didn't it really begin with this feeling of utter exhaustion, with this scent of blood and this thirst, yes, this thirst in the midst of such an expanse of water? Anger destroyed the fabric of their soul and burst forth in an unbearable pain.

To live or die?

They had lost their faces, their names, their tomorrows. They had been emptied of their strength. They had nothing left.

Pokou struggled, unwilling to sink into despair: "No, this is not happening – not to us."

One morning the slaves were all brought up onto the bridge. A frosty sun touched their skin. Nostrils flaring, they breathed in the scent of an unknown land.

Splashed with water, rubbed down and oiled, they trembled with fear. The crew served them double rations.

When they came off the ship and stepped onto foreign ground, it seemed that everything around them – the buildings, the men, the trees – screamed their separation. They had arrived.

What punishment? What curse? What sin deserved such a brutal rending?

With time, their bodies asserted their will: they drank when their throat was parched; ate when hunger demanded it; slept when exhaustion required it; worked until the body could do no more. They chased away the memories that had become agony, they moved beyond the suffering. Mournful songs.

No more sacred forest. No masks. No mystery. Deprived of the seed handed down through the generations, deprived of the protection of the ancestors, the fields were nothing but land to till, vast prison cells.

The slave with the proud brow – Abraha Pokou – still taught her son, now grown into a man, the words she retained of the language from before. Her memory began to awaken, counting out the recollections one by one, like a rosary of precious stones. But a dark shadow fell over her spirit when she remembered the great betrayal. Why had they been sold? Why had they been condemned to such suffering, all for a few guns and trinkets?

The slaves stood alone before their fate; alone before the white masters.

Solitude never left their side, pushing them ever on toward the precipice. They needed to find the strength to overcome the violence that threatened to swallow them up. Not to let themselves be carried away by it. Always trying to do what seemed impossible: to find a bit of love, friendship, or tenderness. Above and beyond all else, to keep dreaming of the great return passage.

One day, like a heavy stone, a child fell from Abraha Pokou's belly. A boy of mixed blood, the colour of sand and straw. He grew at her side, a parasitic plant, devouring his mother's unwilling love and the affection of his brother, who, according to the whispers, was born a prince.

White-skinned God. Immaculate angels. Black devil.

What purpose did the suffering serve?

Would a saviour come one day to deliver them from evil?

Time was lost. The dead had left the living behind. The ancestors were consumed by forgetfulness. New beliefs took hold.

Rebellion was an ever-present temptation, its promise of freedom more beautiful than the rewards of submission. To grab hold of violence and leap into the void. Not to die without having fought, without having stood up to the danger. To struggle on.

Pokou raised her sons to refuse oppression. She taught them not to accept life as it was.

To plan insurrection! To chant the words of revolt:

> *I am a black slave,*
> *I will take up arms*
> *And shoot!*
> *I will not go to Heaven,*
> *But that matters not to me.*
> *I'll go to Hell!*
> *That's where my friends are found!*
> *I am a black slave,*
> *I will take up arms*
> *And shoot!*
> *I may die*
> *But that matters not to me*
> *What I want is liberty!*

Pokou's two sons lived tortured by a deep desire to rebel. They had nothing. They were nothing. They expected nothing. The starkness of their days was unbearable.

And what was ordained came to pass: they discovered the plantation's cache of arms and made off with the guns and pistols. They distributed the arms to the other slaves and, together, they attacked. Having killed the master, his wife and children, they burned down the great house and destroyed the symbols of white power. They ran across the plantation, knocking on all the doors and enjoining the slaves to flee. Jumping on horseback, Pokou's sons escaped with their mother towards the mountains.

But the alarm had already been raised. Plantation owners from the surrounding area hunted down most of the slaves; they were captured or shot dead. Dogs sunk their fangs into the flesh of those who fell.

Abraha Pokou's two sons were captured and hanged, their bodies dragged through the dust of the neighbouring fields.

Later, legend will say that a handful of men and women managed to escape and establish a maroon colony on the sides of a mountain covered with trees.

The story of their escape is still told to this day.

At nightfall, Abraha Pokou, a mother bereft and so alone, sang out her lamentations:

My soul has travelled far.
My eyes have seen every morning,
I have been tossed about, tossed about,
Like a ship on stormy seas.
My ancestors have forsaken me.
Where will my bones be buried?
My soul has travelled far.
I have been tossed about, tossed about,
Like a ship on stormy seas.
But today at last I taste
The sweet fruits of freedom.

Oh freedom, so sweet, so bitter!
I have given everything for you.

Pokou held out her open hands in a gesture of offering. For was she not a healer, an earth-mother, guardian of the most ancient of sufferings?

The Queen Pulled
from the Waters

Stopped by the waters of the Comoé river, whose dull reflections hid crocodiles and hippopotami, the fugitives gathered together to listen to the diviner and the commands of the high priest, the keeper of secrets.

When the nature of the sacrifice demanded by the spirit of the waters was revealed to them, they stood petrified by fear. Then, slowly, all eyes turned to Abraha Pokou.

She would have wanted to scream, but her tongue remained glued to the roof of her mouth. Her throat was on fire. Despite herself, words managed to escape from her lips, although she did not hear them nor understand their meaning. Yet they would forever change the course of her life.

From then on, Pokou gave herself up to the will of others, letting herself be carried away, led on towards the destiny they had shaped for her; a destiny sewn with suffering.

The body of the sacrificial child disappeared down into the dark waters and the people, dumbstruck, saw the river split in two. A strip of dry, virginal land appeared, wending its way to the opposite shore.

The faithful walked between the watery walls.

Once the last man at the end of the column had passed

through, the waters reunited in a torrential roar. It seemed as if the river would leave its bed and spill furiously over the land. Yet it simply resumed its flow, rocked by the rhythms of time eternal.

After having led the people to the land of freedom, Pokou collapsed. None dared to look her in the eyes.

The high priest went towards her and gently lifted her up. Then, turning to the faithful, in a thundering voice he ordered them to kneel down before their queen. They did so, lowering their heads.

Only when Pokou seemed to have risen above her suffering did the fugitives resume their march towards the promised land.

The atmosphere had changed. Now songs rose up, laughter burst out more frequently, words were lighter, faces more serene.

For seven times seven days, they marched through a forest thick but welcoming, clearing a path through so many strange and unfamiliar plants. The spongy ground cushioned their now confident steps. Sweet smells enchanted them. When the light disappeared behind the thick foliage of the towering trees, the men set up camp. In this land of refuge, life was already good.

Yet the tenacity of the queen had not diminished. She wanted to continue marching on quickly – oh so quickly – as if they were still pursued by the Ashanti army, and agreed only reluctantly to stop and rest. The nights brought her no respite, for she spent them with her eyes wide open – the darkness behind her closed lids more frightening than the screams of the forest animals.

Because she refused to sleep, Pokou's mind began to falter. She rambled, at times mumbling to herself, at times screaming at the top of her lungs. For hours at a time she'd go on, speaking to no one save herself.

The queen spoke of power and sacrifice: "The child is dead, the child is dead!" she screamed, shaking her head back and forth violently.

Her body had already lost most of its feminine curves. Emaciated by the exodus, she was so worn out that she often stumbled. When the faithful asked to stop and rest, because the oldest among them were slowing down and the young ones were crying, she would scream: "The child is dead! Are you so spineless that you cannot even stand up to your own weariness?" Staring them down, she added, "Death would be too sweet for you. I curse the day you proclaimed me your queen!" And then she'd begin to weep, burying her face in her hands.

One evening, as she lay on her makeshift bed, Pokou was drenched with sweat. Her teeth chattered and her brow burned. She arched her back, kicked wildly into empty space and screamed.

The healer could not break her fever.

Pokou's niece, whom many saw as her adoptive daughter, tried to comfort her: "Be reassured, the child will return. You know very well that his soul cannot stray far from the family. I feel it flutter and float all around us. You know very well it will not leave the clan. Your son will be born again in one of us."

Seeing that the queen did not react, she continued: "Yesterday evening I spread ashes in front of your shelter. This morning I discovered little footprints there. I assure you, he is trying to come back."

Pokou remained inconsolable.

The high priest proclaimed the truth for all to hear:

"The spirit of the deceased prince is troubling our queen. He is harassing her, trying to garner all her attention. He has turned into a tyrant. Feeling lonely in the world beyond, he wants her to join him. All the Baoule people bear the weight of his displeasure."

Having spoken these words, he addressed the child directly:

"Little Prince, what is it you want? What are you looking for? Do you not see our distraught faces and your mother, crying in despair? Do you not think that we would have done

43

otherwise if we could have? Each one among us feels great remorse. We had hoped to see you one day seated on the throne.

"You two were inseparable. Do you not think that your mother would have acted differently if she could have? Harass her no more – do not add to her suffering.

"Listen to us, her torment must end!"

The faithful decided to act, to make peace between Pokou and her son, and to bring solace to this weeping woman, their beloved queen.

Among them was a sculptor of great reputation. He was charged with creating a small statue, an effigy of the little prince who had been sacrificed.

Putting the very best of his art into this work, the sculptor would imbue it with a force so evocative, so great that it would succeed in opening a pathway between the world of men and that of the spirits. In this way the child would not fail to hear his mother calling out to him.

But before beginning his work, the talented man listened carefully to the queen. She told him of her son, of the image of him that she still kept in her heart, and of her as yet unfulfilled desire to see him again one day.

The sculptor went deep into the forest, looking for a tree whose wood could express the nobility and innocence of the infant. Not one of those hard woods, so difficult to bring to life, which split once the sculpture is finished. Nor one of those capricious woods with a warm side, which brings good luck, and a cold side, bearing ill. No, he wanted a tender wood, of a rare kind.

He had been told to work patiently, in order to allow the child to reveal its presence in the sculpture as it came into being.

The statuette that he finally showed everyone was noble and refined, carved from the very heart of the tree: a pure face, a full and well-shaped body, smooth black skin bearing small ritual scars. The sculptor had produced an exceptional work of art.

The high priest intoned words of welcome as he poured libation on the ground:

Since your departure
There has not been any peace
In your mother's heart,
Nor in the heart of your people.
We hear only cries.
So accept our libation and drink!
We hope that sadness will depart.
So accept our libation and drink!

Abraha Pokou was given the statuette wrapped in a piece of cotton cloth. She carefully uncovered the figure and gazed at it. Her face lit up. She recognised her child.

Left alone, she placed the figure in front of a black pot containing two little white eggs: "Here is your food, eat. I'll give you all you want. I'll give you something to drink. I will take care of you – always."

The queen never again left the statuette, the embodiment of her lost son. She pampered it, running her hands over its limbs again and again, taking such pleasure in feeling the smoothness of the wonderfully polished wood. She caressed the object so much that soon it took on a beautiful patina. You would have said that the statuette was breathing, softly breathing, and that its breath was sweet. Pokou's gestures were imbued with great tenderness.

She no longer felt alone. She was no longer that long-suffering Pokou, but rather Pokou, the fulfilled mother. In her dreams the child came to visit her.

From then on, the queen woke easily, filled with serenity. Peace, at last.

Now that she felt better, they could resume their march. With the statuette slipped inside her wrapper, held close against her body, her gait was confident again, her posture haughty. Strength returned once more to her gaze.

The column's progress was interrupted by pauses for ritual ceremonies. The fugitives left offerings all along their path, so as to obtain the protection of the forest spirits. Monkeys swung from branch to branch, following the trail of those walking, accompanying them with their whoops and warning cries: "Do not come here and destroy the delicate balance of our world. Do not bring ruin and greed with you. Hold back your will to conquer!"

And then one morning, the long-awaited sight appeared.

In front of them, a vast clearing.

The tender green grass, the trees heavy with ripe fruit, and the chirping of birds thrilled the senses. Just then, a herd of elephants moved calmly across the field, their huge ears waving in rhythm with their steps.

"This land is rich – ripe for life," said the oracle. "There are wild yams, palm oil trees, and raffia. Here we shall stay!"

On behalf of them all, the high priest asked the spirits that dwelt there for permission to settle on their land. Once the offerings were accepted, he pronounced the ritual words of thanks: "We thank you for your hospitality and your generosity. You bestow much good upon us by lifting the curse from our lives. We will strive to prove our gratitude and our respect to you."

In that very place, the people raised a new settlement, built a new life for themselves and found hope.

In that very place, Queen Pokou founded the Baoule Kingdom, whose influence spread, extending far beyond its natural boundaries.

In the Claws of Power

While the young women of her generation were busy with their new roles as wives and mothers, Pokou preferred to listen to the public debates and, discreetly, to study the actions of the men. Her character had grown hard. She felt ready to take charge of her own destiny, for no one seemed concerned with her future.

Men were uncomfortable in her presence. Few among them dared to return her gaze, and most thought her body too muscular for a woman. Where was the fleshy fullness? Where were the rolls around her waist where strands of pearls could hide?

By refusing to take part in games of seduction, Pokou became known as cold and inaccessible.

Chastity became a way of life for the young woman, even though it flew in the face of all of society's rules.

Yet Karim, a merchant from the desert lands, found the words of love to tame her. He wore magnificent white *boubous* when he came to call on her, laden with presents from faraway countries. With him, Pokou discovered that a man could still surprise and captivate her.

One day, he murmured to her in his deep voice, his sweet voice, that she would be his queen, his obsession: "I will go deep into you and bring forth the child you have been awaiting for so many dry seasons. When I plunge my eyes into yours, I know exactly where your pleasure is hiding."

He reached out his hand to touch her and saw that she did not pull away, but rather seemed to soften under the pressure of his fingers.

So he continued: "Woman, no man has understood your beauty, the rich flavour of your body. Since I met you, I have longed for only one thing: to let you savour the full force of my devotion."

He became the lover whose existence she admitted to no one, although he was the father of her child – that child she so passionately desired.

No questions were asked. The happiness of the mother-to-be was enough. In any event, the baby belonged to her family line.

And when the time came for the exodus to begin, Karim agreed without hesitation to serve as a guide for Pokou and her partisans. His many trips from the north to the south meant he had the most experience.

And yet he was unaware that in the regions where they were headed, the rainy season had been exceptionally heavy, making the Comoé river impossible to cross.

At the end of a long and exhausting march through the forest, the fugitives arrived before the river. They thought they had fallen into a trap: "The merchant tricked us by leading us here. He wants to lead us to our death! We never should have put our lives into his hands. Pokou misjudged him."

The people roared with anger and frustration.

The high priest tried to calm the crowd.

He asserted that the sacrifice of an infant could save them.

Pokou was already advancing slowly, pushing her son before her. Her face bore a terrifying expression. Struggling, the little boy toddled on.

Karim screamed: "Stop! In the name of Allah, the All Powerful!"

Pokou ordered him to be silent at once.

The people were growing impatient.

She asked for a few minutes to talk with him. But as soon as they drew aside, the merchant spoke first:

"Abraha, you know very well that life is sacred. It is God's gift to us, and only He has the right to take it away. How long did you wait for this child? The diviners don't always hold the truth. I beg of you, don't commit an irreparable sin!"

But Karim's beliefs were not shared by Pokou. For her, his interference was an unacceptable affront.

"Just who are you to speak out openly against the will of the gods? I am the child's mother and I love him. But you need to know that he does not belong to me. He belongs to the people. Do you see all of them there on the shore? They have been pushed to the limits of their strength and they are waiting for me. I must make this sacrifice to save them. I am Abraha Pokou, descendant of a royal line. New lands await us on the other shore of the river. I cannot abuse the hope placed in me. Do not try to shake my determination!"

"Haven't you done enough already? Haven't you already given all that you had for the sake of your people?"

Ignoring his question, Pokou snapped: "I do not care what you think! One can never give enough. I must make this sacrifice, no one can stop me!"

"Not even me?"

"Not even you ... "

"I won't let you do such a thing!" he cried again. "I helped you all because I believed in your cause, but now, I don't want to go on any longer. This child is mine as well, have you forgotten that?"

"Be quiet! If we could stand up against the king's army, our warriors would already be on the battlefield. But you know full well that we have no chance of winning this war. The gods alone can help us. We will do what they ask. You, too, shall bow to their will!" Pokou paused. "Do not push me too far!" she continued, staring him right in the eyes.

"Is that a threat?" asked Karim, stunned by the brutality of her tone.

"Take it as you will. But be very careful. Whatever the bonds between us, I will never let you go against our traditions. My gratitude to you stops there. Move away, I am accountable to my people and to them alone!"

Seeing that her supporters were again showing signs of impatience, Pokou turned her back on him and headed toward a rock overhanging the river. A woman held the child out to her. She took a firm hold of his hand as she scanned the tumultuous waves. The light reflecting off the water blinded her. Her thoughts were leading her in a direction she did not want to take. It was now impossible for her to resist the power that so cruelly offered itself up to her. Death must once again cast its pall over them. The bodies that littered the path of their exodus did not suffice to calm the appetite of the gods. The wheezing of the sick, the cries of the wounded had not been enough to please them. The suffering of the past had not been able to diminish their tyranny.

She was afraid to let go of her child's hand. He started to cry and flail his arms, frightened by his mother's behaviour.

She ought to have expected such intransigence from the gods. Their constant bargaining and their deadly meddling in the affairs of men were well known. Still, she never would have believed that one day they would ask her to sacrifice her own son. Hadn't she always honoured them, fulfilling the traditional rites? Was this the price she had to pay to become queen?

Power is always shown wearing a grimacing mask.

Pokou had long craved power. She had moved towards it, step by step, with determination, knowing that one day she would have to give up everything else for it. Now, it was hers to seize – it was there, right in front of her. It was her destiny to become queen. The oracle had foretold it, the diviner had seen it, the people wished for it.

Never again would a man share her bed. Never again would a child come to rattle her determination. She would not hesitate to eliminate all those who threatened her authority.

It is said that a woman can only reach the pinnacle of power by refusing motherhood.

Is that why Pokou sacrificed her child?

Fear of the gaping female sex, of its moistness, of the blood that lies between life and death.

Any man who dares to steal a glimpse of the shadowy birth canal, the secret of all beginnings, risks death.

When women take off their clothes to dance naked beneath the sky, they do it in order to conjure bad luck, to call forth the spirits of life.

Yes, it had come to this. Pokou would never again be the same:

> *The thickest blood*
> *Is human blood.*
> *The reddest blood,*
> *The strongest smelling,*
> *Is human blood.*
> *Blood is power.*
> *The greatest sacrifice*
> *Is a human sacrifice.*
> *The ultimate sacrifice is that of a child.*

The merchant was bound and dragged off into the forest, where his throat was slit. The boy, it bears repeating, was thrown into the waters of the river.

The Words of the Poet

Legend, too, says the poet, has a mythic dimension. Was the river actually a river? Was the enemy army not in some sense this flood tide in which Pokou and her partisans were about to drown? The king's soldiers, ready to overrun them, to crush them and make their lungs explode: weren't they perhaps a figure for the mud at the bottom of the river that would swallow up those trying to cross?

Everything is possible in legend; those beautiful words created to pacify the people and renew their confidence in the future.

And the child? Was he really a child? Was he not rather the symbol of all that the people held most dear but needed to give up, to abandon, in order to open up a path through the ranks of that powerful army?

Pokou's faithful shivered with fear. Their enemies were poised to attack. Muscles tensed, they were ready to let their arrows fly, to throw their spears, to unsheathe their knives.

The triumphant monarch wanted the complete destruction of the rebels; to destroy their present and their future. More than their century-old treasure, more than the sacred throne, more than the sacred relics, he wanted the irrefutable proof of their submission. How could he know for sure? He needed the very symbol of the people: the child, heir to the throne.

Did they abandon him to the hands of this king, so thirsty for vengeance?

It is also possible that the sacrificed child was not Pokou's son, but one of her young nephews.

And if it were in fact the child of a slave?

Would that have changed the destiny of the people?

Maybe there was no child at all, but rather a young man, a generous soul who had accepted the sacrifice of his own free will, convinced that he was giving his life to save the others.

With his eyes wide open, his breath laboured, his heart thumping and hands trembling, he would have offered up his body to the famished gods.

And what about this extraordinary event that happened right afterwards? The hippopotami rising up out of the water to form a bridge – is that not the symbolic image of a peace treaty; of the King agreeing to let Pokou's partisans live? Magnanimity. The monarch's victory was all the greater for it.

Pokou, free at last to lead her people into exile. Pokou the negotiator, strong because she had succeeded in preventing a blood bath.

Legend still holds secret the key to this sacrifice whose nature eludes us.

The elders are there to help us clear memory's field. The initiates know its full breadth, but they always resist revealing its mysteries. So many among them have died, carrying their secrets away with them, thus closing the doors to the past.

Today, the legend has lost its magical power, and is nothing more than an object of cold and hollow beauty. The words, of course, remain pleasant to hear, but they have also grown dangerous, turning around in the air, here and there, unsure of where to land. They are as sharp as blades. They sink into the minds of school children who recite the tragic story of this mother without understanding the meaning of her sacrifice.

54

Children in the midst of war. Tomorrow, child-soldiers.

Thus, in the deepest recesses of our unconsciousness, and deprived of its sap, the myth follows its own path.

What we see when we dare to take a closer look at ourselves, when we dare to stare into the magma of our becoming, is truly frightful.

The myth emerged too soon from its hiding place. It was unwrapped in haste. It was disfigured, denatured, leaving us forever the poorer, cut off from a much richer knowledge.

III

The Time of the
Bird-Child

The child spreads his wings and flies.

He soars up high, higher still, until he touches the sky. Two fingers from the sun, his iridescent face shines with beauty.

The sun does not burn him, does not split him apart.

The bird-child floats above the countryside, looking at all below. The land is ablaze, swarms of men moan and cry. He sees them beseech the gods, imploring their clemency:

He would want
To erase the fear and devastation,
To wipe the brows of those who suffer.
To float above the Earth,
Above the seas and oceans.

The bird-child spreads his wings, but no one sees him.
No one is aware that he exists.
Yet he has come to fight against ever-present ills.
Tears flow, blood spatters.
He hears everything: the cries, the pleas,
The noise of weapons drowning out human voices.
He smells the stench of hatred, the perfume of fear.

The bird-child flies high over the cliffs
And the expanses of the desert.
He has the power to astonish us,
The power to renew himself.
He never stops in his advance,

The future is always on his side,
Even as the others are only
Babbling the first words of their existence.

He lays the blame on Death itself, and speaks to it with disdain:

"You thought you could suppress me as you have done the best among us, reducing their bodies to dust. You wanted to prevent us from keeping their memory alive, but you will not succeed. I am different now and I will no longer be silent. I have grown, my wings have sprouted, my power has revealed itself. If you can see me, you know that my head touches the sky and that I breathe in the clouds.

"Man, woman, bird. I am the old man, born of the young man. I am the young man, son of the child. Born of the bush and the forest, of the thronging city."

He lowers his eyes and looks once more at the land.

A long black snake slithers on the ground, hides in the tall grass, and then reappears, ready to strike.

The serpent sneaks into houses, bites the inhabitants, re-emerges and heads off into the crowds in the marketplaces, wherever people gather. And they fall, suffering horribly, without knowing why, caught by surprise in the bright light. The land is in ruins, the buildings crumble and fall.

Amulets, ritual phrases, and magic charms are impotent. And all that corrupts has ensconced itself in the hearts of men.

High above, the bird-child glides, circling around and around over the animal whose scales shine in the sunlight. Then, in a flash, he swoops down.

He is as heavy as a mountain.

The snake twists, trying to escape; he hisses and spits out his venom, but he is bolted to the ground, powerless.

And the bird-child laughs, lifting his arms up to the sky.

He has vanquished the Beast.

Véronique Tadjo: Writing across literary, geographic and linguistic borders

A recurrent motif in Véronique Tadjo's life and her work is that of border-crossing. She has crisscrossed the globe in her travels—from Africa to Europe, North America and Asia— and consistently seeks to challenge both accepted generic boundaries and accepted truths in her artistic work. In a recent interview with Bernard Magnier, Tadjo alluded to the importance of her travels for her writing: "I can almost associate each of my texts with a little flag. Each text is marked by the place in which I wrote it. I borrow and incorporate a number of elements gleaned here and there, much like a collector bringing back souvenirs from her trips" (Magnier). Tadjo is a novelist, a poet, an essayist and perhaps most important, an educator. She is also a painter. Images of her artwork accompany recent editions of her writing, including both this translation and the original French edition of *Queen Pokou* (*Reine Pokou: Concerto pour un sacrifice*, Actes Sud, 2004). A spate of recent publications on both sides of the Atlantic makes it clear that Tadjo is receiving considerable and deserved, critical attention for her work. Her growing international stature was recognized in 2005 when she received Le Grand Prix littéraire d'Afrique Noire for *Reine Pokou,* a work that not only challenges the arbitrary borders between literary genres but, more significantly, invites readers to reconsider the ethical and aesthetic implications of the stories and histories we take for granted.

Born in Paris and raised in Abidjan, Tadjo holds a doctorate in African-American Studies from the Sorbonne-Paris IV. She has given seminars and taught at universities from Abidjan to Washington, DC. She currently resides in Johannesburg, South Africa and is Head of French Studies at the University of the Witwatersrand. Since publishing her first collection of poetry, *Latérite* (Hatier, 1984), she has produced in turn works of short and long fiction, modern folk tales, poems, children's literature and essays. She has also edited two anthologies of Sub-Saharan African literature. Still, Tadjo, herself, eschews generic categories, preferring to classify her works as "'texts' ('récits' in French, that is to say, pieces of writing whose genre is not defined)" ("Writing and Its Mis/Fortunes" 1). However categorized, Tadjo's work has attracted a global readership, with translations available in English and an array of other languages, from Spanish and Swedish to Finnish and Vietnamese. In tandem with her writing, Tadjo devotes considerable energy to her work as a visual artist. The illustrations that adorn *La Chanson de la vie* (1989), a collection of modern folk tales published as part of a series for young readers, are more than mere decoration; her artwork opens an interpretive space for children and adults alike, inviting readers not only to explore the meanings and lessons implicit in the stories, but also to refigure them in their own ways. Two of Tadjo's novels, *A Vol d'Oiseau* (Nathan, 1986; l'Harmattan, 1992) and *Champs de bataille et d'amour* (Présence Africaine/ Nouvelles Editions Ivoiriennes, 1993), have been read as examples of contemporary African feminist writing (see, for example, Harrow, *Less than One and Double: A Feminist Reading of African Women's Writing* and Rice-Maximin, "'Nouvelle écriture' from the Ivory Coast: A Reading of Véronique Tadjo's *A Vol d'oiseau*), but her work that has garnered the most critical attention is *L'Ombre d'Imana: Voyages jusqu'au bout du Rwanda* (2000) [translated as *The Shadow of Imana: Travels in the Heart of Rwanda*, by Véronique Wakerley, (Heinemann, 2002)]. *L'Ombre d'Imana*—a memoir of Tadjo's travels to Rwanda after the genocide and her contribution to the collective writing project *Ecrire par devoir de mémoire*—stages a confrontation between personal testimony and collective memory. It reminds us all that the Rwandan genocide is not something that happened 'there' and 'to them', but a global and intimate tragedy that confronts us with the very definition of our shared humanity.

Tadjo's engagement of her reader in an active dialog is, for me, one of the most compelling aspects of her work. Recent critical assessments of Tadjo's work have focused on this ethical dimension of her writing, exploring how she challenges not only our perception of the world around us, but also how we interact with *l'autre,* with our fellow human beings (see, for example, Migraine-George, "L'Autre dans *Champs de bataille et d'amour* de Véronique Tadjo," and Hitchcott, "Travels in Inhumanity: Véronique Tadjo's Tourism in Rwanda"). In *Queen Pokou,* Tadjo pursues her conversation with her reader on two distinct levels, one highly personal, one broadly social. The historic frame of the founding of the Baoule people by Abraha Pokou in the 18th century allows Tadjo to explore not only the most intimate of relationships, that between mother and child, but also the Trans-Atlantic Slave Trade and, ultimately, to reflect on the devastating wars that engulfed West Africa at the end of the 20th century. Written in a style at once enchantingly poetic and deceptively simple, *Queen Pokou* invites readers to approach it on their own terms and from their own perspective. Rather than purporting to provide an historically accurate rendering of how the Baoule came to settle in present-day Côte d'Ivoire, the work's multiple retellings of the story of Abraha Pokou open avenues for discussion about both the past and the challenges of the present, including the sources of ethnic violence and the plight of child soldiers. More to the point, in this work Tadjo asks her readers both to identify with Pokou as a woman—a sister, a mother, a lover, a leader—and to connect the dots that link this historical story to our daily lives and our future.

When she published the first French edition of *Queen Pokou* in 2004, Côte d'Ivoire was still reeling from a devastating period of political instability and civil war. For Tadjo, it was as if the very borders of her country had shifted, locking her out: "Things changed with the Ivorian crisis. I had the impression the door suddenly closed and left me outside. I found it difficult to understand what was happening, how we got there. I felt alienated, as if everything had to be started all over again. I believe that exile begins when you can no longer return to the country you left behind, when the way back becomes painful. But somehow, I think that many Ivorians felt the same thing. This idea that the change was irremediable. The feeling that nothing will ever be the same" (Magnier). Following the death, in late 1993, of President Félix Houphouët-Boigny, who had led the country since its independence from France in 1960, Côte d'Ivoire was plunged into what has proved to be an extended battle for political control. Although Houphouët-Boigny, a member of the Baoule nobility, had previously drawn on the story of Abraha Pokou's sacrifice in order to bolster his own authority, as the country's economy fell into crisis, political leaders played upon the country's ethnic and religious divides to disastrous effect.[8] Even before Houphouët-Boigny's death, Prime Minister Allasane Ouattara had begun identifying and taxing immigrants and guest workers in the country. Then, in advance of the scheduled 1995 elections, Houphouët-Boigny's successor, Henri Konan Bédié, introduced a policy of 'Ivoirité', an ethnically limited definition of national identity that demonised both foreigners and members of Côte d'Ivoire's northern, and predominantly Muslim, minorities; accompanying reforms to the electoral code effectively prevented Ouattara, who has family ties in Burkina Faso, from running for the presidency. The Bédié government fell in 1999 in a coup orchestrated by General Guéi. Elections the following year,

---

8   For detailed analyses of the political situation in Côte d'Ivoire at the turn of the century, including discussions of the concept of "Ivoirité" and of how ethnic tensions were exploited in the post-Houphouët period by political leaders including President Henri Konan Bédié and General Robert Guéi, see the articles by Daddieh, Kouadio, and Yéré.

although marred by the exclusion of numerous opposition candidates and low voter turn-out, ended the General's rule and installed Laurent Gbagbo as president. The government's brutal response to another coup attempt in 2002 led to civil war and the effective division of the country in two, along geographic and ethnic lines: the north and west were controlled by various groups that came together as the "New Forces," while the rest of the country remained under government control. Unfortunately, internationally brokered accords and power-sharing agreements failed to meet their timetables for demilitarisation and for the political reintegration of the country. Elections were repeatedly deferred, even after the signing of the Ouagadougou Political Agreement in 2007, which brought Guillaume Soro, leader of the New Forces opposition group, into the government of President Gbagbo. As of June 2009, when this essay was written, the process of voter registration continues and elections have again been re-scheduled.

While this political context is clearly important for the genesis and reception of *Queen Pokou*, Tadjo's motivation for revisiting the story is less about setting the record straight than about reminding readers of the necessarily permeable border between legend and history, fictional truth and truthful fiction. Tadjo had, in fact, been inhabited by the story of Abraha Pokou and the Baoule migration for quite some time. The opening section of *Queen Pokou* grounds the story and its multiple retellings in the narrator's personal experience; the story she first heard as a young child and that later resurfaced as a side-note in a school history book, resonated quite differently with her when, as an adult, she faced a world redefined by political violence and unbridled personal ambition. In 2000 she published "La légende d'Abla Pokou, reine baoulé" [trans: "The Legend of Abla Pokou, Queen of the Baoule People"], a short story that would later be incorporated into the novel. By making evident the gaps in the historical record—something marked visually by the blank spaces in the short story and the novel— and by asking readers to consider the many "what ifs" glossed over in the familiar story of Abraha (or Abla) Pokou, Tadjo underscores not only the symbolic violence that is done when oral traditions are reduced to political allegory, but also how this process in turn both obscures and justifies very real and brutal acts of violence. As the author explained to me in an e-mail exchange on 13 June, 2008, "[T]he richness of Pokou's legend is that it reminds us, as we are caught up in the wave of xenophobia, that the Baoule people themselves came from beyond the borders of Côte d'Ivoire. In this way, the legend carries within it, in some sense, its own negation" ("re: Abla Pokou").

By contesting established readings of Abraha Pokou's story, Tadjo does more than re-appropriate this one specific foundational story. In the very powerful conclusion of "The Words of the Poet," she insists upon the value of open-ended stories—myths, legends, oral traditions, testimonies and fictions—that bring us face-to-face with our flawed humanity.

In this light, *Queen Pokou* needs to be read both as a personal account of Tadjo's efforts to find a way back across the border to the Côte d'Ivoire where she was raised and as a road map she offers to guide her readers toward the wisdom embedded in the oral tales and foundational stories we know well and too often fail to interrogate. My hope is that this translation will make it possible for more readers to follow the paths Tadjo traces, to re-examine the borders of our humanity and the stories—both personal and shared—that shape our understandings of self and other.

Amy Baram Reid

Translator's Note:

I would like to thank all of those whose support made it possible for this translation to come to fruition. First and foremost, let me offer my heartfelt thanks to Véronique Tadjo. While I alone am responsible for any infelicities in the rendering, I want to acknowledge my great debt to Véronique for her patience, unwavering support and generous advice. She read successive drafts of the translation and consistently pushed me not only to find *le mot juste*, but to develop my own register for the work's poetry. Our Publisher, Nana Ayebia Clarke, has been most supportive; her enthusiasm for the project was clear from the outset and her dedication allowed the book to move quickly through the editorial process. A grant from the Provost's Office and the New College Foundation Faculty Development Fund enabled me to focus on the translation during the summer of 2008 and my colleague, Erin Dean, provided useful feedback on the afterword. Most of all, I am ever grateful for the support and encouragement of my family, in particular, my husband Uzi, who read and discussed the work with me at each stage of the project. Grappling with the many implications of the story of Pokou's sacrifice has made me all the more appreciative of the love, laughter and hugs of our children, Jacob, Miriam and Benjamin and more appreciative, too, of the sustaining influence of my parents, Paul and Lois Reid.

Amy Baram Reid
New College of Florida
Sarasota, 2009.

Works Cited

Daddieh, Cyril K. "Elections and Ethnic Violence in Côte d'Ivoire: The Unfinished Business of Succession and Democratic Transition." *Ethnicity and Recent Democratic Experiments in Africa. African Issues*, 29 (1/2) 2007: 14–10. 11 September, 2008. http://www.jstor.org/stable/1167104

Harrow, Kenneth W. *Less than One and Double: A Feminist Reading of African Women's Writing.* Portsmouth, NH: Heinemann, 2002.

Hitchcott, Nikki. "Travels in Inhumanity: Véronique Tadjo's Tourism in Rwanda." *French Cultural Studies.* 2009; 20: 149–164.

Kouadio, Bertin K. "Democratic experiment in Africa: How Côte d'Ivoire became victim of the civil war" 19 September, 2008. http://democracy- africa.org/africando%202007/ presentations/ bertin_kouadio_paper.doc

Magnier, Bernard. Interview: "Véronique Tadjo, a collector of travel souvenirs." *The UNESCO Courrier*, 2008, no. 2. 22 June, 2009. http://portal.unesco.org/en/ev.phpURL_ID=41752&URL_DO=DO_TOPIC&URL_SECTION=201.html

Migraine-George, Thérèse. « 'L'Autre' dans *Champs de bataille et d'amour* de Véronique Tadjo. » *Women in French Studies*, vol 15 (2007): 67–83.

Rice-Maximin, Micheline. "'Nouvelle écriture' from the Ivory Coast: A Reading of Véronique Tadjo's *A Vol d'oiseau." Postcolonial Subjects: Francophone Women Writers.* Ed. Mary Jean Green, Karen Gould, Micheline Rice-Maximin, Keith L. Walker, and Jack A. Yeager. Minneapolis: U of Minnesota P, 1996. 157–172.

Tadjo, Véronique. « La légende d'Abla Pokou, reine baoulé. » *La Nouvelle Revue Française*, no. 553, May 2000: 197–206. Trans. « The Legend of Abla Pokou, Queen of the Baoulé People, » Amy Baram Reid. *From Africa: New Francophone Stories*, ed. Adele King. Lincoln : U Nebraska Press, 2004. 8–15.

—— *A Vol d'oiseau*. Paris: Nathan, 1986.

—— *La Chanson de la vie*. Paris: CEDA, 1989.

—— *Champs de bataille et d'amour*. Paris/Abidjan: Présence Africaine, Les Nouvelles Editions Ivoiriennes, 1993

—— *Chasing the Sun: Stories from Africa*. London: A & C Black, 2006.

—— *Latérite*. Paris: Hatier, 1984.

—— *L'Ombre d'Imana: Voyages jusqu'au bout du* Rwanda. Arles: Actes Sud, 2000. Trans. *The Shadow of Imana: Travels in the Heart of Rwanda*, Véronique. Wakerley. London: Heinemann, 2002.

—— *Reine Pokou: Concerto pour un sacrifice*. Arles: Actes Sud, 2004.

—— « re: Abla Pokou » e-mail 13 June, 2008.

—— *Talking Drums*. London: A & C Black, 2000.

—— "Writing and Its Mis/Fortunes: How I Write Where I Write." Paper presented as part of a panel organized by the International Writing Program at the University of Iowa, 27 October, 2006. July 01, 2009. http://www.uiowa.edu/~iwp/EVEN/documents/tadjo/final.10.26.realfinal.pdf

Yéré, Henri-Michel. « Reconfiguring Nationhood in Côte d'Ivoire » *Perspectives on Côte d'Ivoire: Between Political Breakdown and Post-Conflict Peace*. Ed. Cyril I. Obi. Discussion papers 39. Uppsala, Sweden: Noriska Afrikainstitutet, 2007. 50–65.

Other Publications by Véronique Tadjo

Latérite (Paris: Hatier, 1984), won the literary prize of the Agence de Coopération Culturelle et Technique in 1983.

A Vol d'Oiseau and *Le Royaume Aveugle*
(both Paris: l'Harmattan, 1992).

Champs de Bataille et d'Amour (Paris/Abidjan: Présence Africaine / Les Nouvelles Editions Ivoiriennes, 1999).

A mi-chemin, her second collection of poems
(Paris: L'Harmattan, 2000).

L'ombre d'Imana, Voyages jusqu'au bout du Rwanda
(Arles: Actes Sud, 2000).

Reine Pokou: Concerto pour un sacrifice (Arles: Actes Sud, 2004).

As The Crow Flies (2001) and *The Shadow of Imana, Travels in the heart of Rwanda (2002)* are published by Heinemann African Writers Series.

Red Earth/Latérite, a bi-lingual edition of her first collection of poems is published by Eastern Washington University Press, (2006).

The Blind Kingdom is published in the UK by Ayebia Clarke Publishing Ltd (2008) and distributed in the UK by Turnaround Publisher Services at www.turnaround-uk.com and in the US by Lynne Rienner Publishers Inc.